Problems in Research on Community Violence

PARTICIPANTS AT THE THEMIS HOUSE WORKSHOP ON RESEARCH PROBLEMS IN COMMUNITY VIOLENCE

STEPHEN BARATZ, Center for Studies of Metropolitan and Regional Mental Health Problems, National Institute of Mental Health, Washington, D.C.

RICHARD BERK, Johns Hopkins University, Baltimore, Md.

DAVID BOESEL, Johns Hopkins University, Baltimore, Md.

ROBERT C. BRICTSON, Systems Development Corporation, Santa Monica, Calif.

HARRY P. CAIN, Center for Studies of Metropolitan and Regional Mental Health Problems, National Institute of Mental Health, Washington, D.C.

NATHAN S. CAPLAN, University of Michigan, Ann Arbor, Mich.

AUDREY CONANT, Lemberg Center, Brandeis University, Waltham, Mass.

RALPH W. CONANT, Lemberg Center, Brandeis University, Waltham, Mass.

NORMAN ELKIN, Director of Urban Planning, Leo J. Shapiro Associates Inc., Chicago, Ill.

RICHARD FISCHER, Lemberg Center, Brandeis University, Waltham, Mass.

EDWARD FLYNN, Division of Extramural Research Program, National Institute of Mental Health, Washington, D.C.

ALBERT GOLLIN, Bureau of Social Science Research Inc., Washington, D.C.

DONALD H. KEORIN, Systems Development Corporation, Santa Monica, Calif.

JAMES H. LAUE, U.S. Department of Justice, Washington, D.C.

MOLLY APPLE LEVIN, Lemberg Center, Brandeis University, Waltham, Mass.

SHELDON G. LEVY, University of Michigan, Ann Arbor, Mich.

RALPH LEWIS, Lemberg Center, Brandeis University, Waltham, Mass.

ELLIOT LIEBOW, Mental Health Study Center, National Institute of Mental Health, Washington, D.C.

MARIE LYONS, Lemberg Center, Brandeis University, Waltham, Mass.

CLARK MCPHAIL, University of South Carolina, Columbia, S.C.

GERALD A. MCWORTER, Fisk University, Nashville, Tenn.

LOUIS MASOTTI, Case Western Reserve University, Cleveland, O.

WALTER MILLER, M.I.T.-Harvard Joint Center for Urban Studies, Cambridge, Mass.

JEFFREY PAIGE, University of Michigan, Ann Arbor, Mich.

JOHN PAPAJOHN, Brandeis University, Waltham, Mass.

RICHARD A. PETERSON, Vanderbilt University, Nashville, Tenn.

ENRICO L. QUARANTELLI, Ohio State University, Columbus, O.

PETER H. ROSSI, Johns Hopkins University, Baltimore, Md.

DAVID SEARS, Harvard University, Cambridge, Mass.

JAY SHULMAN, Cornell University, Ithaca, N.Y.

HARLEY SHANDS, Roosevelt Hospital, New York City

BENJAMIN SINGER, University of Western Ontario, London, Ont.

JOHN P. SPIEGEL, Lemberg Center, Brandeis University, Waltham, Mass.

DAVID SWENSON, National Clearinghouse for Mental Health Information, National Institute of Mental Health, Washington, D.C.

CHARLES TILLY, University of Toronto, Toronto, Ont.

JACK WIENER, Center for Studies of Social Problems, National Institute of Mental Health, Washington, D.C.

 PRAEGER SPECIAL STUDIES IN
U.S. ECONOMIC AND SOCIAL DEVELOPMENT

Problems in Research on Community Violence

Edited by

Ralph W. Conant
Molly Apple Levin

Published in cooperation
with the Lemberg Center
for the Study of Violence,
Brandeis University

FREDERICK A. PRAEGER, Publishers
New York · Washington · London

The purpose of the Praeger Special Studies is to make specialized research monographs in U.S. and international economics and politics available to the academic, business, and government communities. For further information, write to the Special Projects Division, Frederick A. Praeger, Publishers, 111 Fourth Avenue, New York, N.Y. 10003.

HV
6477
.T54
1968

FREDERICK A. PRAEGER, PUBLISHERS
111 Fourth Avenue, New York, N.Y. 10003, U.S.A.
5, Cromwell Place, London S.W.7, England

Published in the United States of America in 1969
by Frederick A. Praeger, Inc., Publishers

© 1969 by Brandeis University

Library of Congress Catalog Card Number: 69-19323

Printed in the United States of America

CONTENTS

INTRODUCTION

Ralph W. Conant

The Themis House Workshop on Research Problems in
Community Violence was convened in April, 1968, by the
National Institute of Mental Health and the Lemberg Center
for the Study of Violence at Brandeis University. The workshop was formed to provide an opportunity for a few interested social scientists to explore adaptations of traditional
and new research techniques to the peculiar problems that
arise in investigations into contemporary collective violence
in American cities. Some of the most difficult problems are
those associated with race relations in the United States;
these problems include the communications gap between
blacks and whites, which makes it extremely difficult (if not
impossible) for white interviewers to obtain reliable responses from blacks on social and political issues; the hostility and suspicion that blacks feel toward whites and the
guilt and paternalism that whites feel toward blacks, both of
which interfere with traditional research approaches; the out-
spoken protest of black leaders against white-sponsored research in the ghettos; and the varied problems of training
"grass-root" ghetto residents for research work.

Community violence was not a very popular research
topic among American social scientists until the civil rights
movement of the last decade gave way in the mid-1960's to
spontaneous widespread rioting in the ghetto communities of
cities.

Although the planned protests of the earlier civil rights
movement have succeeded in achieving some important aims,
primarily through national legislation, the pressures to
exclude the Negro from the white world have remained to
block effectively his channels of upward mobility. Ensuing

frustration in young blacks, unlike that in older generations, has not been repressed. It is indeed constantly seen to result from the harsh realities of Negro life--unemployment and underemployment, inferior schools, and bad housing. It organizes itself into hostile attitudes and beliefs that are vented in angry or deliberate outbursts against the "oppressors"--police, white merchants, and anyone in the "power structure" or "system. "

The rapid increase of massive disorder and chaos has compelled a new public response, and as interest in research on the complexities of the problem quickened, the federal government and other public agencies, private foundations, and social scientists have begun determined (although not concerted) efforts to seek out the questions that should be asked, the methods that might be used to find valid answers, and appropriate mechanisms for translating research findings into community action.

Governmental investigations began with the McCone Commission (Governor's Commission on the Los Angeles Riots) appointed to investigate the Watts riot of 1965. Shortly afterward, the President's Commission on Law Enforcement and Administration of Justice dealt marginally but importantly with some of the conditions underlying community unrest and mass violence. The Newark riot in 1967 brought forth a comprehensive report of the New Jersey Select Commission on Civil Disorder. The President's Commission on Civil Disorder, appointed in the aftermath of the Newark and Detroit disorders of 1967, approached the problem both extensively and intensively and culminated its work with the now familiar report that will serve for many years as policy guidelines for new and improved programs in housing, police and criminal justice, education, employment, community betterment, and black and white relations.

The Presidential Commission on Violence, appointed in 1968 following the assassinations of the Reverend Martin Luther King and Senator Robert F. Kennedy, is at this writing completing its study of the fundamental nature and causes of violent behavior on the part of individuals and whole communities.

An important research role has been played by the
National Institute of Mental Health, which has sponsored and
promoted important projects both within its agency and among
among outside researchers.

Academic researchers in several disciplines, supported
at times by private foundations (the Ford Foundation being
one prominent sponsor) and at times also by governmental
agencies, also have become involved both in theoretical explication and in empirical studies on violence. The Los Angeles
Riot Studies were undertaken by several different researchers
at the University of California at Los Angeles following Watts.
The Detroit and Newark riots have been studied by a number
of different researchers, some based at the University of
Michigan and others working at the University of Western
Ontario, Canada.

The literature on violence has burgeoned with new contributions, notable among them an entire issue of The American Behavioral Scientist (March-April, 1968) devoted to the
subject of urban violence and disorder and an issue of Psychiatric Opinion (June, 1968) dedicated to riot studies, to say
nothing of the numerous single articles both in professional
journals and in the popular press.

Comprehensive empirical studies of disorder are under
way at the Johns Hopkins University, the Survey Research
Center at the University of Michigan, the Disaster Research
Center at Ohio State University, and the Lemberg Center for
the Study of Violence at Brandeis University.

As public and private research has progressed and projects have multiplied, it has become apparent that a systematic and continuous mechanism should be established for
scanning and comparing all the major research efforts. Such
a mechanism would permit researchers to learn from each
other's work; discourage duplication of research; establish
an informal communication among researchers; and provide
research sponsors with an overview of ongoing work in community violence.

The Themis House Workshop was organized to lay the
foundation for such a mechanism. The program of the Workshop focused on three vital areas of concern to researchers:

1. Problems of access to target populations

   a. Ghetto residents
   b. Militant groups
   c. The establishment

2. Research approaches

   a. Opinion and attitude surveys
   b. Experiential surveys
   c. Participant observation
   d. Historical research

3. Special research problems

   a. Sampling
   b. Retrospective and prospective data gathering
   c. Selection and training of interviewers
   d. Interpretation and analysis

The Workshop ran for two days in sequential half-day sessions led respectively by John Spiegel, Director of the Lemberg Center, on problems of access to ghetto populations; Charles Tilly on research approaches; and Peter Rossi on special research problems. This volume is comprised of their presentations and a summary of the discussion that followed each.

The Workshop raised more questions than it answered, but in the process important issues were sorted out for the benefit of researchers and research sponsors. Some of these issues and the primary lessons that were derived from discussion can be summed up as follows.

1. Methodological problems such as those discussed by Charles Tilly (defining the representative phenomena to be studied; dealing with biased enumeration, fragmentary documentation, and multiple units of analysis; and attaching violent action to its context) and the manner in which they are resolved in a research project can seriously affect the outcome of the project, and a deliberate strategy must be developed for dealing with them in individual projects.

x

2. The complexities of community violence, including the vast range of variables, require a multidimensional research approach for a valid analysis. Such an analysis should include both clinical and epidemiological studies because neither approach yields all the major classes of data required to explain empirically the phenomena of collective violence. Although clinical studies maximize the researcher's understanding of the event and participants, they provide little insight into the social and political milieu of the community in which the event was bred. Epidemiological studies, on the other hand, will yield knowledge about underlying social and political causes of community violence without providing clues as to the character of the end result, leaving the researcher or policy-maker in a poor position to recommend an appropriate response.

3. A corollary objective of community violence research should be to find effective methods for distinguishing critical classes of data from non-critical; collecting critical data efficiently and economically; and sorting, relating, and interpreting data in hand. The methodology is extremely important because existing methods are not only imprecise but expensive and therefore marginally productive.

If the many insights that emerged from the Workshop can be summarized in one statement, it is that validity in collective violence research depends equally on incisive questioning in the forming of hypotheses and meticulous care in choosing appropriate methodologies to test these hypotheses. An elegant methodology applied to indecisive questions is as useless in the service of validity as would be the reverse situation.

Future workshops in community violence research should explore solutions to specific theoretical and methodological problems as they are being applied to current research projects in the field. Thus an exchange of discussion on improvements in theory and research methodology hopefully will be combined with an exchange of information about the ongoing research projects in the field.

ACKNOWLEDGMENTS

The Themis House Workshop was sponsored jointly by the Lemberg Center for the Study of Violence and the Applied Research Branch, Division of Extramural Research Programs, of the National Institute of Mental Health. Edward J. Flynn, Assistant Chief of the Applied Research Branch, originated the idea for the Workshop.

I wish to acknowledge the generous contributions of time and effort by John Spiegel, Charles Tilly, and Peter Rossi in their able presentations, which set the pace and high level of the Workshop discussions.

Problems in Research on Community Violence

CHAPTER **1** PROBLEMS OF
ACCESS TO TARGET
POPULATIONS

John P. Spiegel, M.D.

In discussing problems of access to target populations,
I would like to formulate some general principles about the
problems and their solutions and to illustrate these principles
with examples from two case studies of the problem--one of
them an experience in working with ethnic groups and family
interaction patterns, the other an experience in working with
Negro populations in the ghetto.

The general principles have grown out of the work with
these two populations. Other researchers who have worked
with different populations might formulate principles differently. It is good to establish a model for comparing different
target populations because the problems of the two show some
similarities and some differences.

The topic has been broadened to divide it in three ways:
the problem of first obtaining access to the population; the
problem of eliciting the cooperation of the population; and
the problem of maintaining that cooperation.

Obtaining access--that is to say, establishing a contact
with the subjects--is a different matter from obtaining their
cooperation in gathering data. In any long-range endeavor,
there is a separate problem of maintaining the cooperation.
There are differences between each of these three objectives.

Generally speaking, the first obstacle encountered was
the impersonality of social science research, particularly
research of a survey nature. In large-scale survey research,
there is no prior relationship with any subject, and it is

1

necessary to overcome the impersonal knock-on-the-door coloration. The reaction of the subject varies somewhat with his social class. It is easier to overcome this obstacle with middle-class people who understand the purpose of the survey and more difficult with working-class subjects who tend to look more for a personal relationship before they will enter into a study and who do not see the abstract scientific reasons for yielding access.

Another obstacle was the absence of any positive incentive in the mind of the subject that would cause him to allow access. There is no reward, so to speak, and certainly working-class subjects can see this. This absence of a positive incentive is to be distinguished from the presence of a negative feeling toward cooperation in research.

One can name the negative feelings toward cooperation. Some can be applied generally to research; others are directed toward specific research projects. Generally negative feelings are aroused by inconvenience, by asking a subject to use his time for the researcher's purposes rather than his own, by asking him to be at an inconvenient place at an inconvenient time so that he may be interviewed. One has, therefore, to solve problems of scheduling in an elementary sense.

Another negative feeling that is beginning to appear in ghettos is general hostility to research as exploitative. A comparison of research in ghettos with previous experience with family studies demonstrates that such obstacles are by no means confined to ghetto populations. In a variety of contexts, the researcher is seen as one who will do the research for his own purposes with no reward for the subjects.

There are also specific resistances to certain kinds of research. For example, in family studies where the focus was on mental health and illness, the subject had to expose himself and his family's problems to the investigations of the research group. This is a highly sensitive area, and each research endeavor might have a variety of such sensitive areas that could be interpreted as an invasion of privacy. The trustworthiness of those who receive confidential information and the use to which the information will be put are important considerations.

Finally, there is resistance among some groups toward particular institutions or groups, such as now exists among Negroes toward whites in general, toward middle-class and upper-class people in general, or toward such specific institutions as were found in the family study. Among families in Cambridge and Boston, for example, there was a particular hostility toward Harvard. This hostility is being repeated among ghetto populations, which have relatively low opinions of Harvard, M.I.T., Brandeis, and so on. All the universities in the area tend to be surrounded with some form of negative feeling.

How does one resolve these problems? Is there any general approach to pushing through these kinds of resistances? The obstacle of "impersonality in survey research" seems to be generally dependent upon the image that survey research has in the minds of the public. Here again, there is a class difference. Middle-class people are more likely than working-class people to think that survey research is useful. To some extent, overcoming resistance to this kind of impersonality is a matter of achieving good public relations for the study that one is doing and of finding people who can serve as introducers in specific localities. This was, at least, the Lemberg Center's experience with the Roper survey that was done in our Six-City Study. Some of the resistance among the Negro population was overcome when somebody was found within the community to speak favorably of the survey and its research value.

There are various ways to create positive incentives, the most familiar one being to pay the subject. We at the Lemberg Center did not use this method to solve this problem. We used the method of providing service either to the individual or to the group. A third general form of positive incentive is creation of an identification with the research itself. Can one create, in the mind of the subject, the feeling that his participation in the study is going to be useful for knowledge in general and that the advanced knowledge will benefit him as well as others in time?

The other side of creating positive incentive is neutralizing negative feelings where they exist. One way to accomplish this is to overcome the inconvenience factor by having the researcher pursue the subject at times and places convenient to the subject. General hostility to research or particular hostility to the institution demand specific treatment tailored to the nature of the research.

The first group of studies that illustrate these problems and our experience with them are the studies carried on at Harvard with Florence Kluckholm and John Papajohn on acculturation stress in Italian, Irish, Yankee, and Greek families, all at the working-class level. The research goal was to discover the particular cultural conflicts that developed in these ethnic groups as they underwent the acculturation process from native Italians, Irish, and so on to middle-class Americans. In order to do this, we wanted the opportunity to observe family interaction patterns; thus a member of the research team had to be able to observe family members individually, as well as in the family unit.

The first problem was to gain access to a sample of families. The research design being used called for two different samples, one a sample of what were called "sick" families because they had a patient in treatment, and the other, a sample of "well" families, identified as such mainly because nobody was in treatment. The problem of access to the sick families was solved rather easily: They came through the outpatient clinic of the Children's Hospital in Boston. When families of an Italian, Irish, or other background came there and needed referral to a psychiatric clinic, they were referred to us rather than to the clinic at the hospital.

Access to a group of well families was not so easily obtained. A variety of research case-finding methods had to be elaborated. This was the first exposure to the role of the introducer. Someone had to mediate between the team of researchers, Children's Hospital, the Department of Social Relations, and the target population. That person not only would have to find the target families but also would raise with such families the question of whether or not they would participate in research.

For each of the ethnic groups, a different mode of mediation or a different kind of introducer was found. For the Irish-Americans, for example, public health nurses were used because Boston public health nurses have a large number of working-class Irish in their case loads. We went to the public health stations around the city of Boston, described the nature of our research, and tried to get the public health officials acquainted with the name of our researcher. Nurses were asked whether they had families among their case loads of the type needed for research, and if so, whether they would be willing to broach the subject of participation to such families. To our surprise, a great many of the nurses did identify with the aims of the research, made many suggestions, and indicated specific families that would be suitable for the research. The nurses were then asked to broach the subject to the family, and because the nurses repeatedly visited the family and were respected by them, ready access was obtained.

With Italian-American families, the procedure was more informal. Students in our seminars and people working at the hospital heard about our study and approached us with knowledge of an Italian-American family. If the family seemed to be suitable for our study, the introducer would approach the members about participation. In this way, our complement of Italian-American families was filled.

Yankee families were more difficult to find because working-class Yankee families are not common in the inner city. Appropriate families were finally found by going to settlement houses in various parts of Boston. In one case a Protestant missionary society served as introducer.

For the Greek-American sample, John Papajohn worked through the Greek Orthodox Church hierarchy, outlining the research goals and asking the priests for cooperation in helping to locate suitable families within the congregation. This procedure worked well.

The problem of securing cooperation from the families to whom we now had access required differing emphases for the sick and the well families. The main problem with regard to the sick family was to gain access to the husband. Usually the mother would come to the clinic with the child because of a complaint about the child's behavior. The clinic normally would put both the mother and child in treatment. The husband and the other children in the family had to be accessible for family meetings and other procedures. It was important to persuade first the wife and later the husband of

the need to include the husband in this process. This task
was difficult, but it was accomplished by persuading the husband that the family as a whole had something to do with the
illness of the child. In cases of continued resistance, after
the mother and child had had a number of interviews and a
positive transference situation had been established, we would
suggest that we could not continue if the husband would not
agree to participate in the research, meaning that the patients
would be referred back to the clinic and would not be able to
see our research team again. Such a suggestion served as a
threat because a positive relationship had been built up that
the mother was reluctant to drop. There are probably other
ways in which "threat" can be used.

The problem of gaining the cooperation of the well family
required a different solution. We approached the family, told
them that little was known about the well family though quite
a lot was known about the sick family, and asked whether we
could see how they resolved their problems. We said that we
were especially interested to learn how they lived, because
they had been presented to us as a well family. Families
responded to this flattery with a mixture of feelings. On the
one hand, they felt complimented but also, they felt suspi-
cious of what we might find in the family closet and suspi-
cious of our motives. This experience was helpful for our
later work in the ghettos with people who were decidedly sus-
picious of our motives.

We were surprised at the lack of resistance in these well
families to becoming acquainted with our research aims. We
discovered later that another factor that we had not antici-
pated worked positively to motivate these families. We were
to see them once a week for a year or more, and after a time
we realized that they were lonely and were looking forward
to being visited weekly by people from Harvard and different
backgrounds. Eventually they developed an attachment to our
research team.

Maintaining the relationships provided a new experience
for me with such problems outside a purely clinical context.
My previous experience in maintaining sick families in long-
term research dealt mainly with helping the family to solve
problems with the child and demonstrating that some pro-
gress was being made. With well families, it was a different

matter. For scientific purposes, we did not want to change anything in the well families; we wanted only to observe them. However, we found that when the families discovered our backgrounds and experiences, they asked for social services from the team. For example, a family might ask the team to help get a child into a summer camp. We did not feel that we should withhold such services, and so we provided various types of assistance to the families.

Well families developed positive attachments to the research team, and this led to another problem. How does one terminate research when such a relationship has built up with a research subject? This raised in acute form for the first time the problem of exploitation and selfishness on the part of the researcher. Our investment in the project was over, but the family had a different set of expectations. In some cases, the problem was resolved by a simple explanation that the research period was ended and the team would no longer appear. With other families, the contact had to be attenuated over a period of time to avoid a negative image either of the institutions, Harvard and Children's Hospital, or of this kind of research.

It is interesting to compare these experiences with ethnic families and acculturation stress with experiences in gaining access to ghetto populations. The Lemberg Center Six-City and Ten-City Study involved three different populations. The survey of 500 blacks and 500 whites in each of the cities was contracted to the Roper Research Associates, and therefore they had more knowledge than the Lemberg staff of problems of access to that population. The second population group was the influentials--the opinion-makers, the mayors, chiefs of police, and so on, including civil rights workers and militants in the ghetto. Lemberg Center interviewers contacted this population and recorded on tape the single interview obtained with each person. The third population was the ghetto dwellers, who were being seen in a participant-observer context by researchers on the staffs of institutions with which the Lemberg Center had affiliation. Such a research-observer group had been established in San Francisco under the direction of Magoroh Maruyama. The method was one of recruiting and training as interviewers people who lived in the neighborhood and knew their way around it.

The current hostility to research in black communities is quite different from the problem met in dealing with the Boston families where no publicity spotlighted the project. At the time of my acculturation studies, none of our subjects had heard of family research and none knew the researchers; thus there was no public relations problem except that resulting from general hostility to Harvard. This fact is important because the image of the researcher in the slums is of general concern.

Other aspects of the image concern researcher "crowding." For example, when picking cities for the Six-City Study, we were asked to avoid Los Angeles because too many researchers were already there. Overcrowding is a problem now in Boston, with all the universities trying to do research in Roxbury.

The other aspect of this general hostility to research on ghetto populations involved the question of who was in control. The question, and indeed complaint, was often interjected: Who was making the major decisions about research aims, objectives, methods, and so forth--black people or white people? Our answer had to be that white people are for the most part making the decisions, at least for the present time. Blacks are, however, participating more and more in the decision-making process, in setting the goals of the research, and in working out methods of achieving more balance in the operation.

With regard to specific hostility to an institution, Brandeis is not much better off than Harvard, M.I.T., and Boston University. It is, however, out of the central city and not quite so visible to people who live there. Brandeis has not done quite as much in the poor neighborhoods as have these other institutions. But it is a Jewish institution, and given a certain amount of anti-Jewish sentiment in the ghetto population, this factor is one that must be overcome.

Assuming hostility to the institution, we originally thought that the best way to start the survey by the Roper staff in the six cities would be to preserve anonymity of research support. The Roper interviewers were instructed to introduce themselves as members of Roper Research Associates and to explain that they were doing a study of how

people feel about problems in the city. They would not mention Brandeis, the Ford Foundation, or any other source of
support. We thought we would keep this out of anybody's con-
sciousness so that we would have as few extraneous factors
to cope with as possible. After some of the interviews had
been carried out, however, we found some detrimental results; the anonymity (that is, the lack of information about the
sponsorship of the research) had a strange effect. In Akron,
a rumor started that the Roper people were working for the
Ku Klux Klan. We then had to take steps to overcome the
rumor. Our friends at National headquarters of the NAACP
and the Urban League put us in touch with local Akron people.
We found that the Urban League had a Sunday morning radio
show there and that this was an effective way to announce the
sponsorship of the research by Brandeis University and to
stop the rumor. We decided that anonymity of research support and background in this type of survey research might not
be a good policy.

Access to black influentials was gained through formal
and informal introducers. Formal introducers came mostly
from contacts we had with national organizations (which put
us in touch with local people), the mayor's office, and the
local Commission on Human Relations. Interviews were
always tape-recorded and their purpose identified.

To gain access to militants and street leaders, an informal method was used. Contacts were provided by a black
member of the Lemberg Center staff, and in this way we were
able to interview militants who would have been inaccessible
to white members of the staff.

The third target population, the ghetto dweller, was contacted by the grass-roots researcher who lived in the ghetto
and who knew his way around. The grass-roots researcher
served both as introducer and interpreter of the research.
He did not label himself as a researcher as he talked with
people on the street, on the subway, in pool halls, or in bar-
ber shops. In fact, he did not reveal that he was interviewing at all. He held a conversation, a natural dialogue. He
wrote up the interview later and turned it in to us. Not all
such interviews, however, were handled this way. Some of
them were tape-recorded, and of course the interviewer had
to announce to the subject the purpose, sponsorship, and use

of the interview. There was, therefore, a stream of interpretation going back into the ghetto.

To maintain motivation with the influentials and with the ghetto dwellers, we found ourselves providing service on occasion. For example, a group of semidelinquent youths in one city announced to our researcher that they would riot on the weekend. They had three complaints, two of them involving garbage collection and street lights. We interpreted this message as a probe on their part to see whether we would maintain academic aloofness and use the information for our own purposes or whether we would somehow intervene. Our team had a conference and decided to go back and ask the youngsters whether or not we could be of help in establishing a liaison with someone in the city to whom the complaints could be funneled. They welcomed this approach, and we set up a conference between the youths and a person who operated a central communications and exchange post in the city. He heard their complaints and then channeled them to city hall, where some action was taken.

With influentials, especially on the national scene, we have provided some service of this kind. Some of these national figures, black nationalist groups, and so on, have been brought to the Lemberg Center as consultants or for conferences. On the way, they had the opportunity to meet with colleagues from other cities and to hold conferences that were important to them but not important to our research. In this way, we provided a service that was meaningful to the maintenance of a positive relationship and was the equivalent of the social service provided to the well families in the earlier Harvard studies.

The problem of maintaining positive relationships with population groups was found to be a long-term one that became more difficult to solve with time. Researchers must be more flexible, more innovative in dealing with the problem of resistance to research in general and to institutions in particular. Ways must be found to meet the new objections.

SUMMARY OF DISCUSSION

The discussion of John Spiegel's chapter will center on the validity of certain techniques for gaining access to populations.

Effect of the Prevailing Ideology
in the Research Center

Some basic questions may be raised concerning the interviewers themselves. Were they not a fourth population to be considered (with Spiegel's "three-population" analysis)? According to Spiegel, the staff was, in a sense, a microcosm of the influences in the other populations. The staff raised the same questions as the outside populations. Should they continue to work with the Center? What use would be made of the information? All the black personnel at the Center were militant in orientation, and this fact eased the group interaction among them. There was still strain among varying black members of the team because of their individual orientations and there was a certain amount of rivalry for prestige, and so on. But they were all militants, and there were not two opposing camps.

With regard to research results, another question is whether such results can be skewed because of a nonrepresentative prevailing ideology or orientation of the research center, its directors, and its personnel. Furthermore, how can the Lemberg Center's research data be representative when the interviewers were admittedly all militants whose access might have been largely to militants in a community that was largely nonmilitant? There is a risk of getting the easiest and best access to the more militant aspects of the community, who may represent a minority, and thus there is also a risk of badly skewing the data toward the sentiments, practices, attitudes, and so on of this particular group.

Ironically, a person with easy access to a particular group often will suppress what information he gets, or will color it. Cross-checking of information by different interviewers thus reveals gaps or inconsistencies in the data. Interviewers who identify themselves as militants often in fact are ambivalent and will take on the coloration of their surroundings, becoming more militant or more conservative with the company they find themselves in. The more conservative elements of the community are easier to get at; it is the small, far-out element to which access is difficult. Therefore, having interviewers who may be able to establish contact with this small group is costly, and may or may not yield a result.

As noted by John Spiegel, the Lemberg Center has gone on record publicly in favor of social change in general and in favor of the aims of the Black Power Movement. This public image has not hindered the Center in obtaining interviews with rightist white elements, nor has the Center had difficulty in obtaining interviews with influentials in city administration. However, Spiegel did not explain the effect on access to black influentials of having all black militant interviewers.

The same problem of representation is encountered when answers to questions are sharply divided along the lines of some demographic difference in the population. For example, if all Catholics in a sample answer that they will not participate in a riot and all Muslims answer that they will participate, what precautions can be taken in advance to assure that the sample reflects the true proportions of each ideology in the community?

Another access problem related to the attitude of the interviewer toward the survey instrument is that if the interviewer feels that the instrument involved is an imposition, then he or she will get more refusals. Because the interviewee is not aware of the content until after the interview, the interviewer's reaction to the content establishes his rapport with the person he is to interview. However, if the respondent is not enjoying the interview as it proceeds, the attitude of the interviewer toward the survey begins to deteriorate and results also in a higher refusal rate.

Use of Introducers

The effectiveness of national moderate black organizations varies from time to time; many groups that might have been used a year or two ago as effective introducers in local ghettos are no longer useful. In addition, cities vary in the extent to which the NAACP, Urban League, or CORE are influential with their black populations.

Confidential Material

There is no legal protection from subpoena in court proceedings for data obtained in research. There seem to be two techniques for offsetting this vulnerability. One research center instructed its staff to destroy data as soon as possible so that no individual could be identified. Where material was subpoenaed before it could be destroyed, the staff privately agreed to take contempt charges rather than give up the material.

"Natural Dialogue" Interviews

The validity and morality of interviews where the interviewer neither identifies himself and the background of his research nor advises the respondent that he is being interviewed are open to question. The issue of the validity of the information garnered in this way is central to the acquisition of data. In general, any dialogue in which one person is concealing something from the other is not a natural dialogue.

The difficulties of interviewing are compounded by a procedure that takes a person from an ideological position, puts him into an open-ended situation, and then, only after his return, has him put down what he has discussed. Severe validity problems are involved in the kind of data that would be obtained through this practice. This problem could be countered by having people of different ideological positions do cross checks. Because every interviewer starts out with some ideology, which may tend to bias his questions and his memory of the answers, the solution must be in cross-checking with people of different ideologies.

This suggested procedure raises another problem: The interviewee then must be identified so that a cross check can be made, and with such identification, a legal no man's land is crossed, where data are taken from an individual and recorded without his consent. Therefore, although the procedure of cross-checking by interviewers of different ideologies is technically a legitimate methodological procedure, it has implications that are not yet controllable.

Seemingly, a pure moral position in this respect cannot be maintained if researchers still hope to get the most valid data.

Another topic subject to debate is whether more biases are generated in data where the research and researcher are anonymous or in data where a clear identification is made.

CHAPTER 2

METHODS FOR THE STUDY OF COLLECTIVE VIOLENCE

Charles Tilly

As I sat down to assemble these thoughts on the study of violence, the bitter news of Martin Luther King's assassination came over my deskside radio. Word of riots, demonstrations, and looting in a dozen American cities began to break in through the music. The news gave me a hopeless feeling about the task at hand: too little, too late, too distant, too cool. That feeling of triviality and irrelevance has not quite left me. The moral worth or practical value of the research procedures discussed here will take a long time to prove themselves. Meanwhile, men destroy each other, heedless of sociologists and research centers. Still, that assassination and its riotous aftermath set an even higher value on any reliable knowledge that can be accumulated concerning violence, individual or collective.

Social scientists have framed their inquiries into collective violence in many different ways. More so than in most discussions of social behavior, the central questions have been the causal ones. Why, how, and under what conditions do men join in violent acts? The question reappears in numberless disguises within the sociologies of war, revolution, conflict, collective behavior, social movements, politics, cities, crime, mental health, and deviance--let alone the corresponding psychologies, anthropologies, or even brands of economics. This fragmentation of the analysis of violence may indicate that it is so pervasive and heterogeneous a phenomenon that no single theory could contain it. Or it may mean that the perfect moment has been reached for a theoretical shakedown. I am not sure which is the case. But a review of methodological alternatives will most certainly help clarify the theoretical alternatives.   That is the point of this discussion.

Social scientists come to the study of collective violence most directly and systematically in their work on war, revolution, civil disorder, and collective behavior.   The literature actually breaks into two parts.   One group of studies might be called clinical.   These studies examine and compare the internal structures and sequences of distinct cases of collective violence.   The event or movement is the basic unit of analysis, its unfolding is the central problem, and the violence itself of secondary importance.   Such studies run from essays in comparative history like Crane Brinton's Anatomy of Revolution or George Rudé's Crowd in History to contemporary studies like Norman Jackman's or S. Frank Miyamoto's treatments of protests in "relocation" centers to theoretical syntheses like Neil J. Smelser's Theory of Collective Behavior.   Here are an abundance of theoretical schemes and richly documented case studies with little comparability from one study to the next, little attention to the problems of making the data comparable, and extraordinarily crude (and sparse) quantitative analysis.

The other type of study might be called epidemiological, in that it examines the incidence of different types of collective violence in terms of time, place, and people involved. From Pitirim A. Sorokin's massive compilations of the 1930's to Rudolph J. Rummel's extensive quantitative work of the 1960's, the explorer of this body of research ends up with a sense of disproportion: bad data, meager theory, ingenious analysis.   Recently, investigators like Ted Gurr have sought to redress the balance between theory and quantitative analysis.   Even Gurr has had to work with dubious data.   Lewis F. Richardson was one of the very few students of collective violence to express any satisfaction with the sample of events he was analyzing, and he made his sample satisfactory only by restricting his attention to the most obvious general features of "deadly quarrels." This literature offers more guidance for the manipulation of data already in hand than it does for the collection of reliable information.   So far, it has produced few results of theoretical importance.

What distinguishes the study of collective violence as a methodological problem? Simply that collective violence is extraordinary, devastating, and ill-bounded. By "extraordinary" is meant sufficiently rare and tabooed that it is hard for an investigator to anticipate its occurrence, observe it objectively, or acquire full and reliable information about it after the fact. It is devastating in its threat to the very persons and social arrangements--routine recording procedures, local elites, agents of social control--best placed to accumulate an account of its development. It is ill-bounded (as compared with aberrant sexual acts, abortions, political corruption, and espionage, which share a number of features with collective violence) in terms of beginning and end, locale, participants, and basic definition. When does a riot start and end? What territory does it involve? Who takes part-- only those who shoot or get shot? How many fist fights must be seen at the edge of a political rally before the rally can be called a riot? Is a civil war an instance of collective violence or a great many instances loosely linked to each other? Replying that these are purely arbitrary matters makes the point precisely: Collective violence is an exceptionally ill-bounded phenomenon.

Officials and social scientists of Western countries have wrestled successfully with problems much like those involved in the study of collective violence at least once or twice over the last century. The development of uniform crime statistics is a dubious case, because even today many criminologists consider crime statistics nearly worthless as descriptions of the extent and location of criminal behavior. But the accumulated Western experience with industrial strike reporting began with a situation much like that faced by professional observers of civil disorder today.

The strikes of the 1830's and 1840's in England, France, and Germany were extraordinary, devastating, and ill-bounded. That strikes seem less so today is explained to some extent by real changes in their character and to some extent by the growth of a standard vocabulary for their description. More or less simultaneously, durable workers' organizations formed, governments established regular procedures for controlling and recognizing strikes, and a group of analysts specializing in the study of the conduct of strikes emerged. Strikes do not have an intrinsically quantitative character, but a complex set of conventions has grown up for the description of the magnitude and character of strike activity in

Western countries--enough to facilitate meaningful international comparisons. Several of these conventions can be applied with relatively little effort to collective violence. For example, the standard distinctions among measures of magnitude like man-days per striker and strikers per strike provide convenient means of quantifying the differences between big, brief riots and small, long ones. The students of industrial conflict have a number of other practical tips to offer their confreres in the business of collective violence.

One should not exaggerate the case of analogy from industrial conflict. The forms of collective violence that are most like present-day strikes in terms of legality and efficiency of recording--football, automobile racing, and perhaps subway riding--are of no interest to professional students of disorder. Strikes became easier to analyze as they lost some of their extraordinary, devastating, and ill-bounded character.

Anyone dealing with a sort of social behavior that is at once extraordinary, devastating, and ill-bounded can expect to face knotty methodological problems. First are the problems of enumeration and sampling. The combination of extraordinary character and vague boundary means that variations in definitions of relevant events, participants, and so on will significantly affect the results of the analysis. In this respect, the study of collective violence resembles the study of rape more than the study of homicide or voting. Even an omniscient investigator would discover that the particular definition he applied would deeply affect the comparisons he made among regions or social classes.

The mortal social scientist also encounters great difficulty in identifying sources that will permit an unbiased enumeration, and therefore an unbiased sample, of relevant events, participants, and so on--regardless of the definition. He finds some compensation in the tendency of such behavior (1) to attract special attention from mass media, chroniclers, and the like and (2) to encourage the appearance of well-informed individuals who specialize in its detection and control. But he must learn a great deal about their detection procedures and biases before treating their productions as sampling sources.

Second are the problems of documentation. The traces left by extraordinary, devastating, and ill-bounded social phenomena are ordinarily fragmentary, highly selective, and subject to considerable distortion, but rich. Students of such phenomena therefore confront difficulties in assembling reliable uniform descriptions of the cases sampled, especially when the "cases" are events. The same is true when the "cases" are persons, groups, movements, or locales. Most investigators use the lowest common denominator: the body of reliable information that they can bring together for almost every case. That procedure sacrifices the richness of the occasional fragment to the demands of uniformity. If there were a way of linking the well-documented cases to the larger uniform sample, however, it might be possible to retain the advantages of both kinds of data.

Some remedies for the problems of enumeration and documentation come to mind immediately: employing multiple sources for every enumeration of cases; applying several alternative definitions of cases simultaneously in order to be able to compare the effects of definitions; exploiting the records of the agents of social control while introducing some systematic correction for their biases of enumeration and observation; establishing trained observers in likely settings of collective violence and subsequently comparing their enumerations and observations with those appearing in more uniformly and widely available sources. Before rushing to remedies, however, one should think about the more general experiences of students of other extraordinary, devastating, ill-bounded social phenomena.

Mental illness, heresy, natural disaster, and drug use offer good analogies to collective violence in these respects. The difficulties with which social scientists have wrestled in developing systematic accounts of all these extraordinary, devastating, and ill-bounded phenomena have a good deal in common. Students of mental illness have leaned toward epidemiological models and have thus made detection and diagnosis crucial methodological problems. Students of heresy, including political heresy, have vacillated among clinical studies, historical-diffusionist analyses, epidemiology, and attempts to assimilate the problem to more conventional forms of participation and affiliation. Students of disaster have emphasized the investigation of communications (and thereby of the diffusion of beliefs and attitudes); or else they have adopted a simple clinical approach embodied in the question: How do most people react to the news of disaster? Finally, students of drug use have divided sharply between advocates of clinical approaches and defenders of epidemiological analysis.

In brief, we already have considerable experience in dealing with phenomena similar to collective violence. From that experience the following methodological alternatives emerge:

1. Clinical studies following the origins and histories of participants, disturbances, or series of disturbances

2. Epidemiological studies relating units (persons, cities, countries, and so on) involved in collective violence to a larger set of units at risk, as a means of isolating the conditions governing involvement or noninvolvement

3. Participation studies comparing units variously involved in collective violence

4. Diffusion studies concentrating on the sequence and linkage of multiple acts of violence

Clinical and diffusion studies overlap a good deal; so do epidemiological and participation studies. The large choice is between examination of the internal structure of violent events (or persons) and examination of the social conditions producing such events (or persons). Theoretically, the first may well provide some understanding of the way collective violence develops once begun, but it is not likely to have much predictive power. The second may well lead to an understanding of variations in the time and place of collective violence and the people engaged, but it is not likely to yield the means of anticipating the form, sequence, and content of any particular outburst. Practically, the first will most likely suggest therapeutic measures; the second suggests preventive measures. One can, of course, do both. But one cannot easily do both at once.

These observations on methodological choices may be brought together with the earlier conclusions concerning methodological difficulties inherent in the study of collective violence. Three main difficulties were discovered:

1. The sensitivity of the results of the analysis to variations in basic definitions

2. The near impossibility of making an unbiased enumeration of cases, even with a workable definition

3. The fragmentary character of the documentation normally available concerning the full set of relevant cases, which is linked to the sacrifice of richness that follows the restriction of the analysis to those data available in comparable form for most cases

Clearly, these difficulties beset epidemiological analyses more seriously than clinical analyses. Yet to the extent that general patterns are to be inferred from the latter, they become difficulties of clinical analyses as well. The more complex and heterogeneous the phenomenon of collective violence turns out to be, the more likely that numerous comparable cases will be needed in order to infer general patterns. Regardless of which major style of analysis is initially used, effective solutions eventually will have to be developed to all four problems.

Some other variables affect the methods used to investigate collective violence:

1. Unit of analysis

2. Materials available

3. Theory behind the research

Together with the basic style of analysis, these three variables form an interdependent system.

At one time or another, analysts of collective violence have concentrated on all of the following units: events, movements, localities, individuals, and populations.

The Lieberson-Silverman comparison of riot with nonriot cities in the United States, for example, took the locality as its unit of analysis; Stanley Lieberson and Arnold Silverman made no attempt to discover what kinds of individuals take part in riots or why. For the purpose of analyzing precipitants of riots, however, they shifted to the event as the basic unit. Several of the analyses of participation in the Watts riot of 1965, on the other hand, concentrated on the characteristics of individuals apprehended for taking part.

At first glance, the above list might appear to mean that students of collective violence have dealt with every unit they could have dealt with. But the list has one telling lacuna. Analysts of collective violence have rarely, if ever, taken social structures (roles, organizations, networks, families, and so on) as their basic units. The movement, the community, and the social class are about as close as they have come. Most likely this neglect grows from the implicit assumption of a sharp disjunction between collective violence and organized social life.

In any case, the choice among these units deeply affects the character of the investigation. Singling out the locality, for example, commits the investigator to the assumption that local conditions as such somehow affect the character and likelihood of collective violence; this, in turn, makes the bounding of localities and the specification of the relationship between individual and locality into pressing issues of theory and practice. Focusing on the movement (as in the frequent comparison of the American civil rights movement with African nationalism or with nineteenth-century working-class movements) immediately creates the problem of stating the limits and components of such an ill-defined aggregate. And dealing with individuals raises the question of whether or not the relevant effects of relationships and milieu can be adequately represented as individual attributes.

The choice of unit, then, determines to some extent what methodological problems will be most salient. It also determines, or depends on, the choice of theory and data. One of the chief difficulties in recent international comparisons of collective violence is the loose fit among units of analysis, theories, and data. Although the investigators have taken nation-states for comparison, some model of frustration-aggression or deprivation theory that deals with individuals, not nation-states, has commonly guided their thinking. The investigator must, therefore, stretch both theory and method to bring them together.

Of course, in this chaotic field there are often reasons to grab both theory and method wherever they can be found. Sound data on collective violence are hard to come by; their availability may be the most compelling reasons for doing the research a certain way. No taxonomy of data on collective violence yet worked out has much to recommend it. Yet some major characteristics of the available data clearly affect the appropriateness of one method of analysis or another. The following seem to be questions:

1. Do the data mainly describe events of collective violence or units involved in collective violence?

2. Are the descriptions contemporaneous or retrospective?

3. Is the source chiefly recording his (its) own behavior or the behavior of others?

4. Are the data routine by-products of social action or responses elicited by the investigator?

5. Are the accounts of behavior relatively continuous or discontinuous?

With the aid of such questions, one can begin to process data methodically. For example, the first question suggests the following inventory of sources.

A. Mainly describing events of collective violence:

1. Reports of control agents (police, social workers, political officials)

2. Reports of specialist observers, particularly via mass media

3. Testimonies of participants elicited by control agents (interrogations and court proceedings)

B. Mainly describing units involved in collective violence:

    4. Proceedings of formal organizations (city councils, police departments, welfare offices, political associations)

    5. By-products of control activities (police blotters, social agency case records, hospital admission reports, death certificates)

    6. Periodic social accounts (censuses, unemployment statistics, city directories, opinion surveys)

C. Combining accounts of collective violence with descriptions of units involved:

    7. Personal documents (diaries, memoirs, letters, chronicles)

    8. Systematic surveys of participants and nonparticipants

    9. Reports of instructed field observers

If one decides to work chiefly with sources of Type A or B, he sets for himself the hard task of linking sources and/or units. The problem of linking diverse sources of information about the same units arises when one set of sources enumerates the units involved in an action and other sources contain information concerning the characteristics of those units. Sometimes, for example, a researcher has a simple list of persons killed, wounded, and arrested in the course of a disturbance. To make much use of the list, he needs to identify some of the attributes of the persons on it and to attach them to the populations from which they came. Census files, parish registers, city directories, and the like often contain the necessary information. But when the numbers on both sides are large and duplications of names or characteristics frequent, the mechanics of the task become formidable. Nevertheless, the researcher faced with such a problem can find some good leads in the work of demographers (who have often had to bring together information on widely spaced births, deaths, or marriages as these occurred with respect to the same individual or family), urban geographers (who have at times constructed continuous accounts of land use, value, occupancy, and so on for particular plots, blocks, or census tracts), and collective biographers (who have faced the task of assembling comparable life histories for large sets of legislators, aristocrats, or bureaucrats).

Investigators have more experience with the linking of units. In the study of collective violence, the problem arises most often when the sources describing a disturbance or iden- tifying its participants deal with units different from the units dealt with by sources providing information about the back- ground of the disturbance. Frequently, for example, an inves- tigator knows the geography of a disturbance in considerable detail and has good reason to think that the residents of the areas most heavily involved were themselves the chief par- ticipants in the disturbance, but his information on the char- acteristics of areas within the community pertains to larger units like wards or tracts. For some purposes he will have to link the small areas to the larger one by some device such as estimating the proportion of the ward or tract affected by the disturbance.

The investigator faces a similar problem when he has detailed occupational identifications of persons arrested for taking part in a riot, on the one hand, and information con- cerning the wage levels, unemployment rates, or educational levels of major occupational categories, on the other. Again, he will commonly assign the fine occupations to major cate- gories and undertake some sort of calculation of rates of par- ticipation.

The troubles begin when the smaller units do not fit neatly into the larger ones (for example, fine data concerning occupation vs. crude data concerning industry, data concern- ing the ethnic composition of gangs taking part in street fights vs. demographic information concerning areas differing in ethnic composition, and so on). No general remedies are available for such troubles. They have so regularly bedeviled urban sociologists, geographers, analysts of occupational change, and students of public health, however, that the work of specialists in these fields can be illuminating.

Type C sources--those combining accounts of collective violence with descriptions of units involved--do not present the same problems of linkage. Nevertheless, they have their own costs. They rarely appear in archives. Those that do appear (mainly in the forms of memoirs, letters, and other personal documents) are generally unrepresentative of all such records ever produced. Organizations do not routinely generate them. In order to assure their production, a researcher ordinarily needs abundant resources, extensive organization, and considerable prescience. Through field observation and survey procedures, he can assemble such sources only for the present, the future, and the very recent past. To be properly done, the use of personal documents requires great effort and complicated sampling procedures. Type C sources have important advantages in principle, but we must weigh their usually high costs against the alternatives: combinations of Type A and Type B sources via efficient systems of linkage.

The theories behind research into collective violence can be inventoried only in the crudest way. Although the sociologists, economists, political scientists, and psychologists who deal with collective violence lean heavily toward ultimately individualistic explanations, the units about which they theorize are frequently classes, communities, societies, or other groupings larger than the individual. In fact, the fascinating international comparisons conducted by Ivo and Rosalind Feirabend, Bruce M. Russett, Raymond Tanter, Ted Gurr, J. David Singer, and others pose the very delicate issue of applying notions drawn from individual psychology, such as frustration-aggression hypotheses, to the analysis of entire countries. In any case, the central units of available theories of collective violence vary considerably, and these variations have widespread methodological implications.

The time spans of available theories also vary. At the one extreme, extensive theories like those of Barrington Moore or Clark Kerr have related collective violence to very long processes of social change: industrialization, the emergence of new classes, the growth of empires. Only lengthy comparisons of whole societies will provide meaningful tests of those theories. At the other extreme, theories concerning the natural histories of collective outbursts often require only the observation of the time covered by the disturbance itself, and theories concerning the structural conditions inducing collective violence sometimes require barely any time at all for their operation. In the latter cases, observations of short time periods, or even cross-sectional comparisons at a single point in time, will meet the needs of the investigator.

Finally, the central arguments vary. In recent years, four main lines of explanation for collective violence have arisen, singly and in combination: theories of deprivation, social control, power, and aspiration. Deprivation theories trace collective violence to hardships endured by the participants themselves; that deprivation may, of course, be relative to what they have experienced before or to what others in the same society have. Social control theories either emphasize the detachment of individuals from traditional restraints on aggression or protest through mobility, changes in community structure, and so on, or they hypothesize about the decline of effectiveness of elites or specialists in repression; both of these presumably make collective violence easier. Power theories tend to treat collective violence as a part of a more general process of interest-group contention; aspiration theories attribute the rise of collective violence to the spread of new goals, and thus of new dissatisfactions, through some sector of a society. To be sure, most interesting formulations combine two or three of these. Yet the available formulations vary enormously in emphasis; they go from Crane Brinton's stress on the breakdown of social control to James C. Davies' postulated combination of rising aspirations with sudden, short-run deprivation.

Deprivation and aspiration theories easily permit the selection of individuals as the units of analysis. Control and power theories direct attention to larger social units. On the whole, deprivation and aspiration theories present fewer problems of measurement than control and power theories do; changes in the character and effectiveness of social control elude indexing, and estimating the intensity of the struggle for power independently of the extent of collective violence turns out to be hard work indeed. Stated another way, power and aspiration theories direct the researcher's attention to the attitudes, intentions, ideologies, and demands of the people involved in collective violence, and therefore to the collection of personal utterances. Deprivation and control theories turn his attention to the material and social conditions in which they live. Thus varying theories themselves call for varying units, materials, and research procedures.

Such a conclusion makes general rules for the conduct of research on collective violence difficult to establish. Nonetheless it permits a bit more insight concerning the three difficulties inherent in the study of collective violence: the problem of basic definition, the problem of biased enumeration, and the problem of fragmentary documentation. Two more difficulties prevalent in studies of collective violence can now be added: the problem of multiple units of analysis, and the problem of attaching violent action to its context. Much of the technical conversation among students of collective violence over the next few years probably will roam over these five topics. The statements made here will do no more than open the conversation.

THE PROBLEM OF BASIC DEFINITION

The difficulty here is that the definitions applied to collective violence and participation in it strongly affect the results of analysis of collective violence. In this field all definitions have a good measure of arbitrariness to them. In my own work on political disturbances in Europe, the basic definition of the events to be considered is: "An instance of mutual and collective coercion within an autonomous political system which includes violence to persons or property and threatens the existing control over the organized means of coercion within the system."

Appendix A contains a detailed description of the application of this definition to the case of France. Its chief message is that everything depends on the further operations one devises to make the definition work. It was decided, for example, to focus on events in which at least one "formation" (group acting together in the course of the disturbance) had at least fifty members. That numerical minimum became the practical grounds for assuming some threat to the "existing control over the organized means of coercion." Then it turned out that the smaller the disturbance, the less often information was available concerning the number of participants. The problem would have been much more acute with a minimum of fifteen or twenty in a formation, but it was acute enough to make necessary the establishment of a set of

key words like "multitude," "revolt," and so on, whose use
by reporters would, in the absence of numerical information,
qualify the event for inclusion. This procedure was risky and
debatable. In order to identify some of the risks, a further
procedure had to be adopted: "Near misses" were coded and
compared systematically with events that did enter the sample.

Many related difficulties were encountered in deciding
how to bound disturbances with regard to place, time, and
people involved. (Appendix A also outlines some of the ways
of dealing with such difficulties.) One might draw the following general lesson from the experience described here: Because in the study of collective violence the basic definitions
are at once so arbitrary and so crucial, the best procedure
is to work with several alternative definitions of the events
or other units to be considered at the same time and systematically to compare the effects of varying definitions on the
analysis.

Few things illustrate these difficulties better than the
attempt to isolate a set of events called racial disorders.
First, what is a disorder, whether racial or not? How many
people are involved, where, and with what kind of action?
Second, what makes the disorder "racial"? If the identity of
the participants is the index of "race," will disorders involving Indians alone count? If not, will all "multiracial" disorders count, including those with two races fighting on the
same side? Must the disorder be black against white? What
about black against white property? These obvious questions
facilitate the making of some judgment of the intentions of the
participants. But intentions are hard to read in the best of
circumstances. The experience in coding European political
disturbances described above indicates that judgments of the
objectives of various participants are among the least reliable of all judgments. To make the constitution of the basic
sample depend on that sort of judgment is to court disaster.
Therefore, whatever information can be obtained concerning
intentions, ideologies, and sentiments should be recorded
and analyzed, but the inclusion or exclusion of a particular
case should not be made to depend on a judgment of intentions.

THE PROBLEM OF BIASED ENUMERATION

The definitions fundamentally affect the units included, as do the sources available for the enumeration of units. The lower the threshold (in terms of what it takes to include an event, person, place, or period of time in the sample), the more acute the problem. One can therefore mitigate the problem by raising the threshold, at the obvious cost of loss of cases and of generality.

There are other remedies. Instead of employing a high threshold, one can divide a more inclusive sample into several levels of inclusiveness and then conduct the basic analyses separately for each level. If the separate analyses produce substantially the same results, one can probably combine the levels with some confidence. If they produce quite different results, unfortunately, it will be hard to know whether that is because of biased enumeration or because the smaller scale disturbances actually work differently from the large ones.

A third safeguard is to conduct the enumeration independently from more than one source and compare the samples produced. In the study of France, for example, the basic enumeration of disturbances came from the scanning of two Parisian newspapers for each day during the periods under consideration. Lists of disturbances were also prepared from certain long and comprehensive series of police reports in the French national archives and from historical yearbooks that were available for quite a few of the years following the starting point of 1830. Such comparisons discouraged any hope of arriving at the same list of disturbances from these diverse sources, but they did indicate that the newspapers provided the fullest enumeration and that their chief bias was toward the overreporting of events in big cities.

The fourth safeguard--normally a very expensive one-- is to organize one's own enumeration system, to catch the events as they occur. Students of racial disorders in American cities are already experimenting with the organization of teams of skilled observers in ghettos. Their independent enumeration of events, participants, and so forth could provide a valuable check on the biases of cheaper and more

widely applicable means of enumerating units involved in collective violence. It might also be possible to induce organizations already engaged in the detection and control of collective
violence (police departments, gang workers, civil rights
organizations) to collect and provide information according
to standards acceptable to researchers.

THE PROBLEM OF
FRAGMENTARY DOCUMENTATION

There is a dilemma here in that some units provide rich
and idiosyncratic documentation, some provide enough for
systematic comparison with other units, and some provide
almost nothing at all. If the analysis is pushed toward the
richly documented units, either many other cases are jettisoned or comparisons are undertaken that in most cases
provide no information; if the lowest common denominator
is relied upon, a great deal of information is sacrificed.
Some form of multilevel analysis will help meet the difficulty.
Sometimes the investigator can draw a large sample for
which sketchy information can be assembled at low cost.
(If his units are American cities, for instance, he may be
able to assign every city a rough "civil disturbance" score
for a given year and then combine that score with information
already assembled in the card version of the County and City
Data Book.)[1] Then he may be able to afford the drawing of a
small unbiased subsample on which he assembles detailed
information. Three sorts of analysis ensue: crude analyses
of the large sample, fine analyses of the subsample, and
comparisons of the fine and crude analyses for the subsample
alone. This procedure gives the researcher some grounds
for generalizing the results of the fine analysis of the subsample to the entire sample.

Such tactics, however, work only if the investigator can
acquire detailed information on any unit he happens to select.
When his sources hold him prisoner, as is often the case in

---

[1] U.S. Census Bureau, County and City Data Book (Washington, D.C.: Government Printing Office, published annually).

historical work, a multistaged approach will surely help, but
it will not provide a sure means of generalizing from small
sample to large. The best he can do in this case is probably
to define that stratum of his large sample for which detailed
data are likely to be available, draw an unbiased subsample
of that stratum, push for full documentation of that subsample,
and then conduct the three kinds of analyses already mentioned.

THE PROBLEM OF MULTIPLE
UNITS OF ANALYSIS

The difficulty here is that most students of collective
violence are dealing with more than one sort of unit (events,
movements, localities, individuals, or populations) at the
same time. They must reconcile their treatments of the
various units with each other and with the data at hand.
Some ways of linking different kinds of sources to each other
have already been mentioned. The conclusion is rather obvious: One ought not to seek to reduce the analysis to a single type of unit or to devise independent analytic procedures
for each type of unit; rather, one should seek to integrate the
analyses of different types of units with each other. The
researcher who is simultaneously collecting accounts of incidents in a certain city and interviewing a sample of residents
of that city should seek to determine which of the incidents in
his collection most directly affected different members of his
sample and which of his respondents were most directly involved in different incidents. Then he will be able to use each
body of data to amplify the other. In dealing with contemporary collective violence, a combination of survey research,
field observation, and documentary analysis will no doubt pay
off more than a heavy effort directed to only one of these.

THE PROBLEM OF ATTACHING
VIOLENT ACTION TO ITS CONTEXT

The problem of linking violent events to the individuals,
localities, or populations they involve opens up the largest

methodological problem of all: how to represent and measure
the connections which, by our theories, account for the production of a certain variety of collective violence by a certain
kind of social situation.

The problem appears in a small way in the scheme of
stages of racial disorder the Lemberg Center has been using.
The scheme might be diagramed:

PRECIPITATING
      EVENT————→ FRACAS—→CONFRONTATION—→SIEGE
                           ↘ROMAN HOLIDAY

Any such sequential scheme raises a tough question: What
are the probabilities that one stage will actually lead to the
next and that one possible outcome rather than another will
occur? Each of these "stages" has other possible consequences than the diagram represents. To take only the precipitating event, many events comparable to those which
start major racial disorders occur without leading to fracases,
confrontations, or Roman holidays. In order to test theories
that attach considerable importance to the precipitating event,
information must be available concerning the proportion of
all such events that precede racial disorders as well as the
proportion of disorders that begin with such events. This
would, of course, include data on routine arrests, minor
fist fights, and everyday life on the ghetto streets, as well
as the number of potential precipitating events that lead nowhere. On-the-street observation by local teams would help
a great deal; so would the analysis of police blotters and the
review of diaries or time budgets of ghetto dwellers, if they
could be persuaded to keep them.

The same problem assumes much more serious proportions in temporal and ecological analyses of collective violence. Having shown that protest and economic hardship
vary together over time (as argued by R. B. Rose and W. W.
Rostow for example), how can the connection between them
be identified? Statistics show that cities in which Negroes
enjoy little representation in politics and police forces also
have high frequencies of violent protest; but how can the
links between the two variables be specified definitely enough
so that one course of action can be recommended over another?

Evidently by hypothesizing concerning the links and testing for their existence by other forms of research; by giving particularly close attention to the correlates of changes in the variables to which importance is being attributed; by watching for the results of deliberate interventions in those social arrangements when they happen to occur; and perhaps even by manipulating them experimentally and learning whether the effects correspond to our theoretical expectations.

At best, the sort of methodological survey undertaken here sets the agenda and starts the shop talk. This chapter contains little good, practical advice, doubtlessly because the topic of collective violence sprawls, big and awkward, over too large a space. The space has been paced off here in only a preliminary way.

SUMMARY OF DISCUSSION

Five major methodological issues were identified by Dr. Tilly: the problem of basic definition, the problem of biased enumeration, the problem of fragmentary documentation, the problem of multiple units of analysis, and the problem of attaching violent action to its context.

The Problem of Basic Definition

This problem is one of defining what constitutes an instance of violence, civil disorder, or whatever descriptive term is used. The very proliferation of vocabulary in this area indicates that people have trouble with definitions and with deciding what will constitute involvement.

So little is known about the effects of defining either collective violence or involvement that it is necessary to test the effects of the definitions themselves, probably by accumulating methodological experience on what happens to the actual enumeration of participants or events when the definition is changed.

Dr. Tilly amplified his warnings against the use of motive as a criterion in definition:

The conclusion I've drawn from my own work is that the definitions of collective violence had better avoid motives. If you start your work saying, "I'm only going to include those events in which the participants themselves are angry, or are protesting, or are directing their activity against the state or some other group," then it turns out that the most difficult, controversial, inaccessible piece of information is the one that everything depends on, and the alternatives are obviously to use some more readily observable feature of the event or the person to define inclusion or noninclusion in the study. Now this is probably obvious, but it's certainly causing enormous amounts of trouble in

historical and political work on collective violence.
So the great temptation is to begin by defining the
phenomenon itself in terms of the intentions of the
participants, and time and time again this has
undermined the analytic effort because everything
depends on the investigator's initial judgment of
intentions.

Difficulties arise when a population for collective violence research is defined without including information concerning motive in the definition. What are practical measures of definition? One possible criterion for defining
incidents to be included could be whether or not the author-
ities intervened. That could be the test of the seriousness
of an event.

Another is a criterion of scale--using incidents above a
certain size that involved Negroes. Within that group of
events, the research would sort for other variables in which
he was interested, perhaps sorting for incidents that produced
some clear racial content, those of ambiguous racial motivation, and those clearly not racial in intent.

Using formal rather than motivational criteria in the
first sweep of events and then using motivational or other
criteria to further limit inclusion of specific incidents in the
research raises further questions. At what point does one
feed in the additional set of criteria to make the further
limitation, and what kind of criteria can be used to distinguish "collective" violence with some ideological content
from a whole group of collective forms of criminal behavior,
such as the classic gang fights in American cities? How can
one determine, in gang fights involving Negroes and whites,
fine differences between some racial content, routine criminal activity, or mixtures of the two? It is beneficial to "cast
a wide enough net" to pick up such things as gang fights, if
only to help the researcher decide whether or not what he
occasionally labels racial disorder looks very much like
other routine events he would not normally look at.

Moreover, a researcher must have a clear definition of
the population for that set amount of time. After the population is defined, these events have separate attributes: composition, size, important motivation, number of slogans or

observable manifestations. These events may not fall in a
single dimension. Some events might fall primarily on a
racial dimension and others might interact (racial and terri-
torial dimensions, for example).

Problems are involved in using scale as a definitional
criterion. When things are defined as routine, they are not
likely to be reported in newspapers and other obvious sources.
There is thus a close relationship between the data-recover-
ing system and the defining system--the more frequent an
occurrence, the less likely it is to be recorded. This would
demand a very high threshold when scale is used as a criterion of definition. On the other hand, there is no necessary
connection between routineness of an action and lack of some
trace of it. In fact, when disorders or disturbances become
routine, a body of specialists usually develops to record and
deal with them, and the information concerning some routine
disorder or disturbance (such as a labor strike) will most
likely be more reliably recorded and managed than before.

A further consideration is that although routine disturbances may be recorded, the records probably do not concen-
trate on small-scale events. Therefore research requiring
these records would necessitate extensive retrieval work.
The problem could be handled by changing the definition of a
population to exclude small-scale events whose data would
be difficult to recover.

This type of limitation, "threshold manipulation," leads
to the problem of deciding on an appropriate scale for the
particular environment or context of the research. One way
of handling this problem is to index the maximum normal
level of congregation in a community and to use this as a
standard against which to compare any particular incident
within the community. Another possibility, albeit a crude
one, would be to relate the size of the incident to the size of
the community itself if the community were used as a unit of
analysis.

Problems of definition would be easier to solve if they
were considered a function of the researcher's goals. If the
researcher first asked the question of why he was studying
riots, he would find it simpler to define what units he needed
to answer his question.

Scale has something to do with the researcher's foreknow-
ledge of his sample. A researcher who is not on sure ground
must have a larger universe; if he reduces the size of his
sample, he must be sure that it is typical. The word "riot"
has something to do with scale and magnitude of effects, but
hardly anyone is yet sure where to make such cutoffs. One
of the problems of definition is that a researcher often must
deal with events when he has very few conceptual tools for
establishing the delimiting factors.

Sometimes motivation is excluded from the definition;
then, with the formal definition, the researcher generates a
particular population of events and then proceeds to accept
motivation as one of his important variables and to redefine
and re-sort his population. There is little difference between
doing this and starting right off with motivation in a definition.

One way to get around the tricky question of motivation
is to ask how the event is perceived. The consequences of
events are really the results of how they are perceived rather
than what they actually are. Instead of delving into motivation (whether or not an event is motivated by racial considerations) the question could be asked after the fact whether or
not the event was perceived as a racially connected one.

The Problem of Biased Enumeration

Even with a workable definition, most researchers do
not have access to a body of data that permits them to identify
all events or individuals of that kind easily. They are thus
prevented from making a reasonable sampling of all such
events or individuals or other units.

If a research design is built around an enumeration procedure that gets at different populations via different methods,
there will be a risk that the differences between the populations that are measured are not representative of the larger
populations from which the individuals were drawn. That is
to say, different kinds of people are involved in the networks
that are used to gain access to particular populations, and
the network itself strongly influences the information obtained
through it. What if two populations are used for comparative

purposes in a study? Access to one is gained through public
health clinics; access to the other is gained through friendship
or through churches. Is there a systematic difference between
these populations that will interfere with whatever variable
is being tested on both so that, in effect, one winds up testing
characteristics of the populations rather than the variable?
Is it possible that response to an investigator varies systematically with the access network used? The problem relates
also to the earlier discussion of the effect on research results
of the ideology in a research center. For example, has the
use of black militant interviewers and access to black influentials through militant black staff members at the Lemberg
Center resulted in biased enumeration?

One way to check on enumeration is to manipulate the
threshold. This device is used not only to cut down the
amount of information available and the number of cases to
study, but also to make a compromise between the number
of cases that are definitely relatively unbiased and those not
so certainly in this category.

A second alternative is to use more than one means to
enumerate the population and to ascertain on which part of
the population there is agreement between the sources. In
some cases it is possible, by using three or so independent
means of enumerating events, to find out what difference the
source itself makes.

The importance of discovering whether or not a reality
exists outside the perceptions of any event is debatable. A
researcher may be able to proceed with perceptions as his
raw data. However, there must be some consensus as to
what constitutes the true population or events to be studied,
some agreement on approach to enumeration, even though
it is approached through different networks.

The Problem of Fragmentary Documentation

Fragmentary documentation and biased enumeration are
often intertwined problems. What happens when one relies
on the agents of social control themselves (police, social
workers, youth leaders) to provide him with the enumeration

that he needs? What is the experience with putting his own observers in place?

Police department tape recordings of police actions during the nights or times of disturbances have often been found useful; however, this information usually needs to be checked. One form of validation, as was used in a study of the Roxbury riot, was to use interviews with participants and observations about their participation as one body of data and subsequent talks with city officials about their responses to the events as another body of data.

An informal grid system with observers stationed at intervals has also been used to record a chronological record of events. The events were used as a takeoff point for interviews with both control agents and demonstrators. Into this data was fed additional tape-recorded information, such as police calls, to facilitate comprehensive knowledge of these activities. Hopefully, this will eventually become a community-monitoring operation on a continual basis.

Auxiliary sources of manpower for observations and documentation have been local members of the Council of Churches (who were monitoring the nerve center in Roxbury) and newspaper people who were being trained and equipped for faster communication in crises. As their skill and accuracy increased, they became a more important source for establishing chronology in events.

Newspaper reports of mass meetings have not always been a very accurate source of documentation but have been perhaps consistently inaccurate enough to be usable if correction was made for the inaccuracy. In Rochester, the newspapers consistently magnified the number of participants in mass meetings by some 25 to 50 per cent over the last three years, 1965-68. In Memphis, however, newspapers underestimated participation.

Constant observers often have been useful, but the need to employ enough personnel over a long period of time in noncrisis situations so that they could function effectively in crisis situations called for an investment few research organizations were prepared to make.

Another way of getting around fragmentary documentation is to use a subsample of a larger population for which documentation is only fragmentary. The subsample is then analyzed more carefully and in detail, and one can estimate from the results of subsampling what might happen in the larger population if the documentation were more complete.

How useful is survey research? Survey research is considered to be advantageous in obtaining uniform information about whatever unit is being researched. However, survey research is only one useful order of information. Survey research should never be used as an exclusive basis of information about anything. Much survey research is tapping into a body of ritualized sentiment that has very irregular relationships to what people may really think and even more irregular relationships to what they in fact do.

If one recognizes clearly the order of information that is being obtained from the survey research, such information can be extremely useful. But it is dangerous to impute the true range of people's actual sentiments and the true range of relationship between sentiments and behavior to results obtained from survey research alone, despite the fact that survey information more than occasionally conforms with the behavioral observations that one makes.

How accurate is the prediction that is made on the basis of survey research? Probably .6 is a good correlation between those who say they will do something (for example, participate in a riot) and those who actually do it. There is a tendency to overstate the degree to which a person intends to participate in any action.

Nonetheless, it is doubtful that as much could have been learned as quickly in the studies described herein if some method other than survey interviewing had been used.

The Problem of Multiple Units of Analysis

This problem is a particularly tricky one in studies of collective violence because there is interest in the community as a unit, in individuals and how they behave, and in events

and how they occur, each of these forming at some time a
unit of analysis. Dealing with multiple units of analysis of
different levels of complexity often presents no particular
problem methodologically. The only problem is the challenge
that is presented to one's ingenuity.

However, when there are two pools of data, one a description of events, independently collected, and the other a description of individuals, produced by survey research, the
difficulty is to link these two. Whereas there is no problem
in principle, in practice the problem is that these are two
very ill-bounded groups.

In addition to the problem of how the questions are asked,
there is the problem of how to bring together the data collected for the different units--on the one hand, data on the
natural history of riots and, on the other hand, data about
individual participation or involvement from surveys. These
are questions that research groups framing survey applications will have to cope with individually.

How relevant is survey research and what are the relative merits of survey and observation techniques in learning
about riots? The geography of the riot automatically imposes
limitations on the sample. That is, if one is sampling ran-
domly a set of points, where there are peaks of riot activity,
he should be able to determine that riot activity was reported
from those points. Moreover, riot observation is a relatively
random kind of event. The people who observe riotous kinds
of events (looting, arson, sniping) may not be distributed the
same way in which samples are to be taken, resulting in
built-in bias. If one is going to make aggregate observations,
they must be aggregated on the basis of the same kind of
random distribution that the observations of riot events are
going to obtain. One solution to this problem is to weigh the
observations by the quality of the observation. The more
opportunities or the more access the observer has for view-
ing, the more weight his opinions should have.

Attaching Violent Action to Its Context

What kind of incidents precipitate violence? If these
incidents somehow figure importantly in a natural history

scheme, is there any way of predicting which confrontations with the police, out of a large set of events, actually are followed by a riot? These questions will be discussed later in this volume.

CHAPTER **3** SOME ISSUES IN THE
COMPARATIVE STUDY OF
COMMUNITY VIOLENCE

Peter H. Rossi

INTRODUCTION

Although studies of community violence entail special
problems of their own, they must deal with certain chronic
conditions that are also encountered by research directed
toward other community-centered phenomena. Despite the
fact that it is one of the oldest empirical fields in sociology,
community research is still in a primitive stage of development. First, there is little in the way of fruitful theory that
helps to guide the design of investigations into community
phenomena or even to define the relevant aspects of community to which attention should be given. Furthermore, community research is costly in terms of time and resources.
Even the case study of a particular community requires as
much commitment as much larger studies of individuals but
usually yields less in terms of generality of results. Finally,
the data collected in community studies tend to be qualitative
in character, thus presenting special problems in analysis.

The topics to which this study is addressed are related
intimately to the state of impoverishment of community
studies. The first question that will be raised is the most
basic question of community theory: Is the concept of "community" a relevant way of making distinctions among social
phenomena? Secondly, certain limited aspects of data-
collection problems, particularly those arising in the study
of community elites, will be analyzed. Finally, some problems arising in the handling of qualitative data will be considered.

44

This discussion is based largely on firsthand experiences with attempts to design and carry through community research and on the reconstruction of the experiences of others as described in the published literature of community research. It is hoped that this study will aid in the development of the innovations so sorely needed to make community research intellectually respectable, scientific, and less painful to undertake.

SOME CONSIDERATIONS IN THE DESIGN OF COMMUNITY RESEARCH

A basic assumption underlying community research made by those who are committed to community research is that a study of the local community as a unit is a useful and meaningful way of making distinctions in the social world. However, mention of this is made not merely as a rhetorical device to serve as a prelude to an expression of faith in community as concept and community study as a way of life, but because the raising of this question leads to important considerations in research design. Because community research, properly designed, is expensive, community researchers must demonstrate that such research is more productive than alternative and presumably less expensive ways of approaching a particular problem.

Until recently, community studies were undertaken on the assumption that a particular local community (Muncie, Indiana, or Newburyport, Massachusetts, or Biloxi, Mississippi) was a sufficient microcosm of the larger American society and therefore could serve as a reasonable research site for studies of American culture and social structure. Indeed, such studies are still being undertaken, although more modest claims are being made for their generality. At least in the early days of Robert and Helen Lynd and W. Lloyd Warner and his associates, the claim could be made that the technology and funds were not available for making either a large number of community studies or national studies.[1]

---

[1]The main works of the Lynds and Warner and his associates are: Robert S. Lynd and Helen M. Lynd, Middletown

The argument made against generalizing from the findings in a Middletown or a Yankee City arose in large part from the growth of empirical knowledge concerning the ranges of variation in crucial respects that were found in the American population and that were associated with socioeconomic, regional, ethnic, and community size variables. Thus a Middletown or a Yankee City could be different from the rest of American society because the mix of critical population types in those places was different from the mix in the rest of American society. One version of this argument was that the variation from community to community is primarily the result of differing proportions of critical population types that make up the aggregate called the community. This version of argument was a particularly cogent one because the argument made for such community studies was often its converse.[2]

Experiences in research on other types of institutions have also added to the weight of the question of whether or not the concept of community is a useful and meaningful one.[3] Over the past decade, a great deal of effort has gone into the study of variations among schools and colleges, with the end result that most of the variation among such institutions can be ascribed only to the different mixes of students who attend them. Thus Harvard, Brandeis, and Johns Hopkins merely attract and select a more highly talented group than does the

<hr />

(New York: Harcourt, Brace and World, 1929); and Middletown in Transition (New York: Harcourt, Brace and World, 1939). W. Lloyd Warner, et al., The Social Life of a Modern Community (New Haven, Conn.: Yale University Press, 1941). This is the first of a series by the same authors, the last volume of which was published in 1959.

[2]Indeed Muncie, Indiana, was chosen as a research site because it was closest to the median on a large number of community characteristics that included size, location, occupational composition, and racial mixture.

[3]See James S. Coleman, et al., Equality of Educational Opportunity (Washington, D.C.: Government Printing Office, 1966); James A. Davis, Undergraduate Career Decisions and Great Aspirations (Chicago: Aldine Press, 1966).

University of Mudflat or St. John's University. By dint of great effort and some convolutions of data-handling and analysis, it is possible to tease out a "compositional effect," but such effects of the total population of a school tend to be minor compared with the main effects of population mixes. Adolescents coming from families of lower socioeconomic status who attend high schools having high proportions of middle-status students tend to have higher levels of aspiration than do students from families of comparable status who attend schools largely composed of students from the same socioeconomic level. However, the main differences among schools remain associated with the average socioeconomic level of the students recruited.

Considerably more comfort can be gained from studies in which the focus of interest is on community social structure rather than on the behavior of individuals within communities. For example, studies of community decisions to fluoridate water supply indicated that the main difference from community to community was whether or not the decision was put to popular referendum or decided by administrative action.[4] Similarly, desegregation decisions acceptable to Negro civil rights groups were more likely to be made by appointed rather than elected school boards.[5]

These studies suggest that significant amounts of intercommunity variation can be found in the structural characteristics of local configurations and that such structural differences are largely independent of aggregative and compositional effects. ("Structural" here means primarily the actions of such formal political entities as school boards, public health boards, city councils.)[6] Few examples are

---

[4]Robert L. Crain, et al., The Fluoridation Decision: Community Controversy and Innovation (Indianapolis, Indiana: Bobbs-Merril, 1967).

[5]Robert L. Crain, et al., School Desegregation Decisions in the North, Report 110A (Chicago: University of Chicago, National Opinion Research Center, 1966).

[6]A more formal definition of "structural" components is as follows: Community structure includes those formal

available of empirical linkages being made between structural features of a community and collective behavior. Perhaps the best example is a study conducted by Robert Hanson that related successfully the stands taken by officials of local organizations to the popular vote in local referendums. [7]

The major question that arises with respect to community violence is whether or not this is a phenomenon in which major intercommunity differences lie in the aggregated characteristics of each population, in the compositional nature of the community, or in structural features of the community. It seems hardly likely that community violence is entirely structural in character (like the decisions to desegregate school systems). More likely, it is related mainly to aggregative and compositional characteristics, as well as some structural effects. The main reasoning behind such an expectation lies in the fact that community violence is a form of collective behavior, a phenomenon more likely to be related to characteristics of aggregates or compositional factors than to structural factors.

This is not to deny the importance of structural factors but to relegate them to a more subordinate position. Thus

---

organizations whose explicit function it is to make authoritative decisions binding on the total community (local government bodies), and on those organizations at least one of whose main purposes is to affect those decisions (for example, decisions of political parties, neighborhood associations, Parent-Teacher Associations, and minority defense associations). This definition does not include organizations not oriented mainly to the community (business enterprises) or those which do not attempt directly to affect decision-making (families and churches). The purpose of this definition is to focus attention on those elements of the associational life of local communities most closely related to community decision-making. For a more extended discussion of the rationale behind this definition, see Peter H. Rossi, "Community Decision Making," Administrative Science Quarterly, Vol. I (June, 1956).

[7]Robert C. Hanson, "Predicting a Community Decision: A Test of the Miller-Form Hypothesis," American Sociological Review, XXIV (1959), 662-71.

research into intercommunity variation in community violence should be oriented primarily toward characteristics of the populations of the communities in question and only secondarily toward structural features of those communities. Thus present forms of collective violence can be more readily explained in terms of the general position of the Negro components of the populations of communities than in terms of the behavior of public officials, although the latter may have some influence on the form, timing, and extensiveness of community violence.

The word underlined in the last sentence is designed to draw the attention of the reader to the possibility that community violence can take several forms, of which the "present" round of unfortunate events is only one. Up to the present, the breakdown of order in the Negro sections of major cities has appeared to take on more of the aspects of collective behavior than organized protest. There is good reason to expect that as the Negro communities become better organized, civil disorders will be both more controlled and more focused on political goals. In the future rounds of civil disorders (actual or threatened), structural features of local communities undoubtedly will be more important.

The implications of these considerations for the design of research in this area are as follows.

1. Research on community violence must concern itself with the problem of the respective roles held by the aggregated characteristics of the population involved, by compositional factors (the relative proportion of Negroes and whites), and by structural features (the actions of public officials).

2. This implies a data-collection operation that is concerned as much with surveys of the general population, Negro and white, as it is with surveys of elites, Negro and white.

3. The dependent variables should be phrased not merely in terms of whether or not community violence occurred but also in terms of its timing, duration, extensiveness, and resolution.

4. This implies a research design that is compara-
    tive and in which there are two levels of analyses:
    one concerned with the comparative positions of
    Negro and white populations within cities and one
    concerned with intercommunity variation in the
    actions and behavior of elites. It may well be the
    case that all the variation among communities
    can be explained in terms of the first level, with
    the second level being largely irrelevant to whether
    or not riots occur, when they occur, and what
    happens as an aftermath.

5. If one is primarily concerned with the sources of
    intercommunity variation that are associated with
    structural features of local communities, then
    the basic unit of analysis becomes a community.
    The size of a sample then is the number of local
    communities studied. Such a sample size must
    necessarily be fairly large to detect structural
    effects, especially if, as suggested above, such
    structural effects are relatively unimportant.
    Thus a sample size of 10 or 15 or even 20 com-
    munities is small. Sample sizes of 50 to 100
    communities may be more appropriate.

SOME DATA-COLLECTION PROBLEMS

Some part of the effort in studies of community violence
ought to be devoted to an analysis of sample surveys of appropriate populations in a sample of cities. The theory and
practice of sampling human populations within geographic
areas is now so well developed that ways of conducting sample surveys of the Negro and white populations of a sample of
cities will not be discussed here. The major problems in
conducting such sample surveys lie in obtaining access to the
populations involved in carrying through sampling plans in
what has always been a difficult population to sample.

The most immediate problem facing the researcher interested in comparative community research is how to obtain a

reasonably large sample of communities without incurring prohibitive costs. By and large, the costs of sample surveys vary more with the number of interviews conducted than with the size of the universe being sampled or with the number of places within which sampling is taken. It costs very little more (relatively speaking) to conduct a sample of the population of the United States than to take a sample survey of the population of Boston, given the same sample size in both cases. Thus a reasonably well-executed probability sample (of say, 1,500 persons) survey of the United States population would cost somewhere between $75,000 and $100,000, whereas a survey of about the same size of Boston's population would cost around $50,000 to $75,000. In short, two national samples could be taken for about the cost of conducting three local community sample surveys.

The usual solution is to cut the sample size within each community sampled. Thus in the 1967 Survey Research Center (SRC) study of Negro and white populations in 15 cities, the samples drawn were of 200 white and 200 Negro persons within each city. The consequences of employing such small samples within each community are that only the crudest analyses can be made of any particular city, although inter-city differences can be fairly well shown. The design of the SRC study also made it possible to undertake fairly reasonable comparisons between whites and Negroes within each city. The costs of conducting such a survey were around $250,000, a fairly large sum for research these days.

To raise the size of the sample of communities to a reasonably adequate number means that very few comparative community studies are likely to be funded that rely heavily on samples of the general populations within each of the cities being studied. Of course, it is possible to get by with smaller samples within each city if one is willing to give up all but the grossest measures of community differences. More likely, comparative community research is going to proceed through the use of samples of urban populations selected in such a way as to maximize their efficiency in explaining some particular dependent variable. Thus one may pick cities that present strong contrasts with respect to community violence, as was done both in the Lemberg Center's 1966-67 study and in the studies being conducted by the Survey

Research Center and the Johns Hopkins Department of Social Relations under the sponsorship of the National Advisory Commission on Civil Disorders.

This strategy of sampling cities has certain unpleasant features. First, it maximizes the regression effect. Picking any sample of individuals by oversampling the extremes on any continuum results in an increased probability of picking individuals who, by virtue of measurement error and other factors, are artificially extreme. Thus the regression effect would lead to the expectation that cities that did not have riots in some particular year will be especially likely to suffer riots in the future and that cities that have had riots will be less likely to have them in the future.[8] Secondly, small samples lead to overdetermination in explanation. Thus in the Johns Hopkins University study of 15 cities essentially 14 degrees of freedom were available to work with. It is extremely easy to use up 14 degrees of freedom by developing a not-too-complicated theory to explain the patterning of differences among the communities, a theory that is bound not to hold up in replications. Finally, such samples (picked to maximize a particular dependent variable) are likely to be single-purpose studies, good for explaining that particular dependent variable but not very good for anything else.

Unfortunately, no easy solutions are in sight that are feasible in terms of both reducing costs and at least maintaining data quality. The conduct of sample surveys is a labor-intensive activity. All the improvements in sample surveys in the past three decades have raised the degree of labor intensivity. No new developments are in the offing that will lower the direct labor-cost component in surveying, although it is obvious that the pressure is decidedly in the direction of

---

[8]This is exactly what happened in the Johns Hopkins University study. The cities were chosen on the basis of their riot status in 1967, positions that were completely upset by the events of spring, 1968. Thus, of the 5 cities chosen to represent nonriot cities on the basis of their behavior in 1967, 3 (Washington, Baltimore, and Pittsburgh) had severe riots in 1968. Similarly, of the 5 cities chosen to present severe rioting as of 1967, none had severe disturbances in 1968.

providing incentives for cost-saving inventions. In the mean-
time, comparative community investigations that rely on
adequate-sized samples of communities will be few and far
between.

Researchers conducting sample surveys of the general
population are in the contradictory position of knowing what
they ought to do but not being able to command the resources
to carry out their notions of what would be the best possible
procedures to employ. In the case of surveys of elites, researchers are somewhat in the opposite position. They know
only vaguely what they want to do, and if they had more clarity in this respect, such an objective would be relatively easy
to carry out.

The purpose of elite surveys is to obtain data on the
structural level of local communities (at least in this context
of studies of community violence). Elites may be defined as
those persons who, because of their positions or their activities, have considerably more information than usual about
the structural activities in question. The survey of elites in
15 cities mentioned above was concerned with ascertaining,
among other things, the patterns of communications between
public officials and Negro leaders, the degree and kind of
organization to be found within the Negro community, and the
responsiveness of public officials and notables to the demands
of the Negro population within each community. These goals
were not very specific, but they did lead to a conception of a
universe to be sampled that consisted of two types of potential
respondents: those whose own attitudes are to be studied
(public officials whose responsiveness to the Negro community may be analyzed), and those who are in a position to
know what is going on (informants who may provide data concerning the organizational structure of the Negro community).

The universe to be sampled is certainly not clearly
enough defined to permit enumeration of a set of directions
that would enable a reasonably intelligent person to list every
individual who belongs to that universe in a particular community. In contrast, consider the clarity of definition possible in sample surveys of the general population that define
the universe as consisting of all persons within a certain age
range whose usual domicile is within the boundaries of some
geographic area and who are not institutionalized.

In practice, the criteria of belonging to the universes of elites to be sampled are variations on the following. First, all individuals occupying particular positions (mayors, police chiefs, heads of departments of public welfare) fall into the sample. Second, all those individuals who are mentioned by the above as important actors also fall into the universe. Although the application of these two criteria would seem to lead to a great many errors of either Type I (including people who should not be included) or Type II (excluding people who should be included), in practice, this is not likely to be the case. Indeed, if anything, the incidence of Type I errors appears to be more likely than the incidence of Type II errors. Evidence for this statement, although not very firm, may be found in Samuel Stouffer's experiments with replications of the technique. These experiments indicate that there is considerable convergence between independent teams of elite interviewers following general instructions of this sort. Some overlapping studies also indicate a considerable amount of agreement. [9]

The reasons for the success of this technique for identifying elites are not entirely clear. Its success is probably based on several characteristics of elite groups. In any one community, only a small number of people play leadership roles. By virtue of maneuvering to influence each other, the actors rapidly become known to each other; so that if one approaches the central figures in any action, which, by definition, include major public officials, one can rapidly fan out one's knowledge to cover almost everyone who is playing an important role. There seldom are mysterious figures in the typical community and few whose machinations remain unknown to most of the major actors involved.

———————————

[9] Unfortunately, Stouffer's work in this area was not published, his death occurring apparently before his study was ready for publication. Kent M. Jenning's work, Community Influentials (New York: Free Press, 1964), represents a replication in part of Floyd N. Hunter's earlier study of Atlanta, Georgia Community Power Structure (Chapel Hill: University of North Carolina Press, 1953). Although Jenning labors mightily to show how Hunter's modes of procedure affected his substantive results, the careful reader can easily see that there is little difference between the two, especially with regard to the respondents covered by referral techniques.

Obviously the success of elite studies of this sort depends heavily on the skill of the interviewers used. It is possible to designate in advance the public officials and officeholders in major organizations that such a team should start with, but the decisions whether or not to follow up "leads" that develop in the course of interviewing has to be left up to the discretion of team members. A general instruction to follow up every lead would minimize Type II errors but would lead to overinterviewing in most situations.

What sorts of persons should be recruited to form teams for interviewing elites? I have used three types of teams. My most successful experience has been with using myself and one or two colleagues as the interviewers. For example, James A. Davis and I spent a short two weeks in Zanesville, Ohio, and interviewed 60 elite members and 40 members of the general public. Another type of team has been composed of graduate students who were sent out from Chicago to spend a week in each of 16 cities studying desegration decisions made by school board. The students did extremely well in locating and interviewing elite persons, although the quality of their interviews left something to be desired. Finally, in the Johns Hopkins University study of 15 cities, field workers were hired who had been used by the National Advisory Commission on Civil Disorders. These persons came from fairly diverse backgrounds (law students, political science graduate students, former Office of Economic Opportunity workers). Although the final evaluation of their performance has yet to be made, their performance was least satisfactory, a function primarily of the fact that such a team has to act as an extension of the principal investigators' intuitions, more easily acquired by graduate students with whom one has worked closely than by ad hoc groups coming from diverse backgrounds.

If the selection of respondents is a problem, the conduct of such elite interviews is a morass. In survey interviewing, it is possible by structuring the interview instrument to make the course of the interview quite operator-free, although almost everyone who has been interviewed by a survey interviewer has had ample cause to doubt the reliability of any computer run from such surveys. In elite interviewing, it is much more difficult to make the interview situation operator-free. The information to be obtained from each

respondent varies according to his position, and the respondents are ordinarily considerably more articulate than are
members of the general public. How "good" the interviews
are depends very heavily on how sensitive the interviewers
are in probing a particular area, in phrasing questions properly, in defining themselves as knowledgeable persons with
whom one can "level," and so on. Reading the protocols of
such interviews can be a painful experience when one sees
the number of opportunities missed to ask incisive questions
and to obtain additional pertinent information.

In short, it is apparently easy enough to devise a fairly
satisfactory sampling procedure for elite surveying, although
it is more difficult to train a set of interviewers to conduct
interviews in the same manner as the principal investigator
himself would interview in the same situations.

At this point, it may be worthwhile to consider a new
development presently under way at the National Opinion Research Center (NORC) at the University of Chicago. The
Center has selected a probability sample of 200 American
cities with populations of 500,000 and over. The sample con-
sists of all cities in the United States with populations of
150,000 and over and a one-in-three sample of United States
cities with populations of between 50,000 and 150,000. The
sample is designed to remain constant over time. Hence the
name Permanent Community Sample (PCS). [10]

The PCS has two main activities. First, it is a data
bank containing various types of information concerning each
of the cities, obtained from censuses, surveys, documentary
materials (concerning the structure of local government),
and previous social science studies. Secondly, it is a data-
collection apparatus centered around the cities in the sample
that will be available for use by social scientists who are
interested in comparative community studies.

The latter activity would be of most interest in the study
of community violence. The data-collection apparatus will

---

[10]A detailed description of the PCS, along with a discus-
sion of applications, is contained in Peter H. Rossi and
Robert Crain, "The NORC Permanent Community Sample,"
Public Opinion Quarterly (Summer, 1968).

include, in each city, a social scientist who is associated with a local college or university. He will be employed on a part-time basis to maintain a data-collection point for the data bank and to act as a general informant on activities in the city. In addition, a small panel of elites will be recruited to be interviewed periodically concerning local issues. Finally, an interviewer will be selected (or a regular NORC supervisor will be used, if the city is a sampling point in the regular NORC samples) to be trained in elite interviewing so that he will be capable of conducting such interviews on his own and of training a local crew of interviewers to supplement his own activities. The number of such interviewers in any one locale will not be very large--perhaps half a dozen at the most.

There are several advantages to employing a data-collection apparatus of this sort in future comparative studies. First, a major cost in the employment of ad hoc interviewing teams is obviated; it is very expensive to ship out teams from any spot to a reasonable sample of cities. Second, after training, survey interviewers of the caliber of NORC super-visors could be matched with most graduate students in the social sciences (at least as far as interviewing skills are concerned). The data-collection apparatus should be able to produce data of at least as high a quality as ad hoc teams and probably of higher quality than the initial run of interviews coming from ad hoc team operations. Finally, the data bank can be employed to provide additional information of each of the communities studied.

The PCS was used for the first time in a survey of school-board decisions. By the end of 1969, it should be possible to evaluate how successful the operation is. So far, the reports seem to indicate that it is working extremely well. Indeed, many of the interviews approach the quality of those produced by graduate students and have the further advantage of being written in legible handwriting.

A STRATEGY FOR HANDLING
QUALITATIVE DATA

By virtue of the restraints placed upon interviewers by questionnaire schedules and by detailed sampling instructions,

the data generated by sample surveys are relatively simple
to handle. In raw form, responses are choices made among
limited sets of alternatives or in maximum complex form as
short sentences given in response to open-ended questions.
Whatever the defects of sample surveys, they at least have
the advantage of providing raw data in forms that are easily
assimilated by the technology of punch cards, computers,
and survey analysts.

In contrast, the problems presented by the qualitative
interviews conducted with community elites in 15 cities in
the Johns Hopkins University study appear considerably
greater. Here, the interviewers were not furnished with a
schedule but had instead an interview guide that set forth in
outline form the topics interviewers should cover in each
interview, using their judgment as to whether a particular
respondent was to be questioned mainly on one or two topics
(because of his special position or expertise) or whether a
larger set of topics should be broached. Elite respondents
are generally articulate and opinionated individuals who are
not easily led from one topic to another, especially when the
form of the interview is relatively unstructured. As a con-
sequence, the interview protocols, purporting to be recon-
structions of interview situations (made from notes and dic-
tated), vary considerably in coverage, quality, and length,
all characteristics that may or may not closely correlate
with the interactions that actually transpired in the course
of the interviews.

If these interviews had been intended primarily to ferret
out what actually transpired in a particular community (the
course of the civil disorders or the specific actions undertaken by the police department) or if they had been intended
as means for characterizing respondents, not much could
have been done with them because of their unevenness and
unknown reliability. Fortunately, the major concern of the
Johns Hopkins study was not with the reconstruction of actual
events or even with differences among individual respondents
but rather with differences among cities. Differences among
cities in respect to broad variables were more likely to have
been captured by the interviews, even though individuals
might not have been completely reflected in each interview
situation.

Therefore, the decision was made to treat the interviews in the same way that researchers treat similar unreliable and fragmentary materials of the sort that are found in the human relations area files. First of all, interviews were used not to provide information on respondents but to characterize the community in question. Thus, all the information on particular topics from each interview was gathered into data pools for each city. All the references to communications between city officials and Negro civil rights leaders for a particular city were culled from each interview and collated. (The actual physical handling of protocols resulted in folders of excerpts bearing on each topic for each of the 15 cities.)

Second, a number of variables were devised according to what seemed important to distinguish among cities. For example, in order to characterize how responsive the mayor of each city appeared to Negro civil rights leaders, a variable entitled "mayor's responsiveness to civil rights leaders" was distinguished.

Third, raters were used to read the protocol excerpts on each topic and to place the cities in rank order along each of the dimensions to be distinguished. For example, the 15 cities were ranked in terms of the mayor's responsiveness to civil rights leaders, from the most responsive to the least. Disagreements among raters were used to characterize the reliability of a particular dimension and hopefully were ironed out through discussion among raters. At least three raters were employed to accomplish this task.

Finally, the end results were a set of rank orders, one for each of the major dimensions along which the structural features of the cities were contrasted.

Consideration was also given to the employment of data quality controls along the lines discussed by Raoul Naroll. [11] Excerpts from interview protocols would be characterized according to characteristics of the respondent that could be related to the quality of the data produced by the interview with that respondent. For example, an excerpt coming from

---

[11]Raoul Naroll, Data Quality Control (New York: Free Press, 1962).

a respondent who was in a good position to know about the
topic in question would be rated as of higher quality than data
coming from a respondent who was not in such a position.
Thus an excerpt from a Negro civil rights leader making
statements about the access of civil rights leaders to the
mayor would be of better quality than statements from the
white head of the Chamber of Commerce. Restricting the
rating task to data of better quality probably would appreciably
raise the reliability of the rating task. Employment of this
technique would depend on the time and resources available.

Although the main impetus behind the use of this strategy
for handling qualitative data stemmed from a disappointment
with the quality of the interviews, the strategy would be useful to apply to any set of qualitative interviews, with better-
quality interviews producing correspondingly more reliable
ratings. The advantages of such a strategy include relative
objectivity, minimization of the selectivity of analysts, and
provision of the bases for quantitative comparisons among
cities. Obviously, such a strategy would depend heavily on
having enough cases to sustain such an analysis; a number (N)
of 15 would barely make the grade.

There are many more methodological issues in the comparative study of communities than have been touched upon in
this study. The selection principle is of salience to the author
in the midst of a research project, a compound of hindsights
of regret and prospects of solutions.

SUMMARY OF DISCUSSION

The discussion of the points made by Peter Rossi will focus on five central themes: importance of compositional vs. structural effects on violence, understanding the effects of time in changing collective violence, problems in interviewing of elites to gain information on community structure, relative problems of superficiality and extensiveness vs. depth and exclusiveness in data, and problems of research design and choice of variables.

Importance of Compositional vs. Structural Effects on Violence

Dr. Rossi stated that community violence probably is not entirely structural in character but is more likely to be related mainly to aggregative and compositional characteristics, as well as some structural effects. Clearly, the riot is a maturing process in which community structure and community composition or aggregative effects play different roles at different stages of violence.

The initial riot may be largely an effect of the characteristics of the people who riot. However, subsequent disturbances (or the events after the initial riot) are likely to be greatly affected by the structural response or the political response in particular to that first riot. Thus over a period of time, the major source of variants in violence from community to community may be the structural differences in those communities. The response to a riot actually is a continuous thing that is happening before the riot occurs. In this sense, the structural effect becomes important even earlier in the chronology of a riot and its aftermath.

There is a need to study communities over a period of time in order to assess the effects of composition and structure on collective behavior. However, the relative importance of composition or structure in either triggering or preventing collective violence is debatable. Knowledge of the presence of Negroes having certain aggressive characteristics

may more frequently lead to a prediction of a riot than knowledge of what has been going on in that community before.
Researchers often have started out with the view that attitud-
inal and compositional effects were more important than anything else but have ended up with the feeling of constant inter-
action--the attitudes are part of the structure, and the structure is responding to attitudes, so both must be known. Prior
to a first riot, the colinearity seems impossible to unravel.
But following the first riot, structural effects begin to emerge
in a way that enables one possibly to unravel the aggregate or
compositional from the structural effect, and this is likely to
be more the case over time.

If structural effects account for very little variation
among communities, why bother with them? Because if one
is interested in social change, this is the community level
that can be most easily changed and, therefore, is worth
bothering with even if its effect is only minor.

Understanding the Effects of Time
in Changing Collective Violence

The prediction feature of riot theories calls for an understanding of the difference between prevalence and incidence.
Whereas prevalence of riots can only continue to increase,
probability of incidence of riots during some base period will
probably change in time. There is a diffusion factor involved
in that riots are probably a learned behavior, and if the orig-
inal riot had taken some other form, perhaps what is happening in cities throughout the United States would now be in a
form other than riot. Because the riot turned out to be an
effective and dramatic instrument for bringing attention to
the plight of the Negro, it was utilized in community after
community.

The form of riots probably will shift with time. In the
interaction between the occurrence of a riot, the political
structure of the city, and the organization of the Negro community, the riot probably will be transformed from the relatively uncontrolled activity it now is to a more controlled
type of activity to be used directly as a political weapon--a
deterrent weapon. Nevertheless, lacking rapid organization

of the Negro community into controlled behavior, riots might be transformed in time into guerrilla-type Negro-white warfare.

There are difficulties inherent in the measurement of structural effects against a noncontinuous variable such as whether or not a riot occurred. The effects of structural changes may also be obscured by the traumatic nature of a riot and the possibility that it may not be repeated in spite of provocative structural changes.

Are structural and compositional characteristics of a community independently variable or correlated? A case in point may be offered for the independent variability theory. In Rochester, New York, whites have retrogressed in their attitudes toward racial problems, whereas the company on which most of them depend, Eastman Kodak, a central institution in that it is the major employer in Rochester, has changed its relationship to institution-building dramatically in 1968.

Problems in Interviewing of Elites To Gain Information on Community Structure

The question may be raised whether or not samples of elites are systematically biased in that certain elements (the underground crime element for example) are probably inaccessible for interviewing, though they are influential in the community. Such elements are not necessarily inaccessible, though they usually are not identified by occupation.

When an interview team "blitzes" a city for a week or two, asking sensitive, open-ended questions of people unknown to them, there may be serious problems concerning the reliability and completeness of the interviews. Indigenous interviewers are usually desirable, and under the new setup of the Permanent Community Sample being organized by NORC in Chicago, it should eventually be possible to use local interviewers. Are the NORC-type interviewers, the "little old ladies in tennis shoes," sufficiently sensitive and probing to elicit sophisticated elite information? A case can be made for both the graduate students and the ladies. Nowadays, maybe the little old lady is the graduate student.

The problem of quality control of interviews has three main aspects: how to weight the responses of those elites who are judged to be more knowledgeable on a particular process than other elites; how to judge which statements within any one interview are most representative of the respondent's feelings when the interview contains contradictory material; how to maintain quality control on the questions the interviewer asks.

With regard to the first aspect of the problem, the lack of consensus among elites in the community, it may be possible to work with such secondary variables as degree of conflict in the community between blacks and whites, amount of information each elite interviewed may have, and importance in the community of whatever process is under discussion. Quality control checks on the interviewer's questions can be maintained if the interviews are taped. It is more difficult when the interviews are recorded only by abridged notes. Through interviewing the same elites twice a year, as the Lemberg Center hopes to do in its ten cities, the true positions of the respondent may become clear over time. Their changing positions in response to changing policy situations may also be revealed. This method may be too large an undertaking for the usual research organization, but it is organizationally possible and is actually in process of organization at the Lemberg Center.

The validity of ranking cities on the basis of elite information with respect to variants is questionable, because the ranking must be accomplished through qualitative judgments made on internally inconsistent interviews. There is as yet no model to ferret out what a person really means on a particular dimension when he has said three different things. Thus rank one will be clear and rank fifteen will be clear, but there probably will be fuzz in between.

Despite the fact that a clear conception of the dimension is possible and the fact that when the data are finally recovered they can be ordered, these dimensions are not usually closed ahead of time. Elites tend to reject check lists or forced-choice answers, and some elites have more information in some areas than in others. Moreover, the interviewer often is wise to change his questions as he becomes more knowledgeable about the situation he is probing. Still, a researcher might close the questions in a small part of the interview to allow these questions to be controlled and checked, and, at the same time, allow the respondent to range broadly over whatever other topics he had in mind.

Relative Problems of Superficiality and
Extensiveness vs. Depth and
Exclusiveness in Data

Given the importance of doing intercity studies, the critical problem is getting the kind of data crucial to an analysis of process, structure, and composition within the particular cities that make up the sample.

Is it possible to link a natural history clinical model with survey techniques, data banks, and so on, bringing together qualitative data for the individual cities and yet permitting intercity comparisons on a variety of independent variables?

According to Peter Rossi, it is preferable to obtain a sample of superficial and less definite information across a large number of cities rather than to make an in-depth study. Both probably could be done if enough money were available, however. An intensive study of a city or of 4 cities would not definitely yield more information than nonintensive study of 200; fluoridation studies started out on a small scale but led nowhere toward understanding fluoridation controversies until one went to a very extensive sample.

Problem of Research Design
and Choice of Variables

Rossi felt that what is really crucial is the wiggle,[12] which represents certain structural or central institutional

---

[12]"Wiggle" means the response of a social entity (in this case cities) to an occurrence of the sort one is investigating (in this case riots).

characteristics. It may well be possible to take the sample of cities on the basis of the nature of the wiggle rather than on the basis of aggregate characteristics, and this may in the last analysis be a more intelligent design to understand the process of social change than the kind of designs presently available. When a riot occurs in one of these communities, it tends to maximize the wiggle.

Should a research design select cities on the basis of how they respond to a first and a second riot (how they wiggle), with maximization of that variation (involving in the equation the degree to which the black community is organized, what kind of leadership style is predominant, and so on) rather than selecting cities on the basis of aggregated characteristics as now? One problem is the rapidity of change in the community. By the time the community is selected on such a basis and a study launched of black organization or whatever, the organization will be changing.

There are peculiar qualities of cities, qualities inherent in different size, that interfere with valid comparisons between them. For example, New York and Akron are both cities, but they really can't be lumped into the same population. One solution to this problem is to treat the very large cities as a separate universe.

CHAPTER **4** SUMMARY AND
CONCLUSIONS

Ralph W. Conant and Molly Apple Levin

The Themis House Workshop focused on most of the
salient problems of research associated with race-related
violence on the contemporary American scene. The main
areas of concern in the discussions were problems of access
to target populations, alternative methodological approaches,
and problems involved in comparative analysis among communities.

John Spiegel dealt with three aspects of the problem of
access to target populations: (1) obtaining access in the first
place, (2) eliciting cooperation of the population after gaining
access, and (3) maintaining cooperation. Spiegel described
the obstacles to obtaining access as general hostility to research, an attitude among ghetto residents that social science is impersonal and nonproductive, and negative feelings
aroused by inconvenience. In describing his experiences in
previous research on family mental health, he related certain ways to overcome some of the obstacles: use of "introducers" in specific localities to pave the way for favorable
attitudes toward the research and also to gain access to
"influentials" in the black community; creation of such positive incentives as paying a research subject or providing
some useful service for him; neutralizing negative feelings
by overcoming inconvenience.

Spiegel noted the "overcrowding" of researchers in the
field, particularly in large, violence-prone cities, and the
fact that blacks want an increasing role in setting research
goals and carrying them out. Anonymity of research sponsors, he argued, was not the answer. For him, anonymity
raised more problems in the form of rumors than it avoided.

Access to militants and street leaders, Spiegel found, could
be gained through a staff member at the Lemberg Center, and
the man in the street could be reached by indigenous, well-
trained, ghetto dwellers.

In summary, Spiegel felt that the problems of gaining
access to ghetto populations are long-term ones that are
increasingly difficult to resolve. He recommended flexibility
and innovation to overcome resistance.

Charles Tilly dealt with the principal methodological
alternatives for the study of collective violence and the difficulties the researcher encounters in the application.

He cited four alternatives:

1. Clinical studies of the origins and histories of
    participants and the disturbances or series of
    disturbances

2. Epidemiological studies relating the unit studied
    (persons, cities, countries, incidents) to a
    larger set of units as a means of isolating the
    conditions governing involvement or noninvolve-
    ment

3. Participation studies comparing units variously
    involved in collective violence

4. Diffusion studies concentrating on the sequence
    and linkage of multiple acts of violence

The principal difficulties seen by Tilly were:

1. Sensitivity of the analytic results to variations
    in basic definitions

For example, in isolating a set of events called racial
disorders, what is a disorder? How many people are involved, where, and with what kind of action? What makes
the disorder racial? Must it be black against white, and people against people? Does it include attacks on property?
Using motivation of the participants as a definitional criterion, Tilly concluded, is to court disaster, because this

criterion may turn out to be the most difficult piece of information to obtain.

   2. Near impossibility of making an unbiased enumera-
       tion of cases, even with a workable definition

   The sources from which the data are gathered may be
systematically biased and will affect the analysis, particularly if a low threshold for inclusion produces large quantities
of units whose data sources are uncertain. The problem
could be mitigated by manipulation of the threshold at a cost
of loss of cases and of generality. Alternatively, one could
divide the sample into several levels of inclusiveness and
analyze each level separately. If the separate analyses
yielded similar results, one could proceed to combine the
levels with some confidence. If the results were quite different, biased enumeration might be responsible or smaller-
scale disturbances might work differently from the large ones.
A third safeguard would be to conduct the enumeration independently from more than one source and compare the samples produced. A fourth safeguard would be to organize one's
own enumeration system so as to catch the events as they
occur (for instance, with teams of trained ghetto observers
and in units with which researchers are already experimenting). Agencies of social control (police, gang workers,
social workers) might also be induced to collect and provide
information according to preagreed standards.

   3. Fragmentary character of the documentation
       normally available in a full set of relevant cases
       or the sacrifice of richness that follows the
       restriction of the analysis to those data avail-
       able in comparable form for most cases

   Some units of analysis provide rich and idiosyncratic
documentation, some provide enough for systematic comparison with other units, some provide almost nothing. If the
analysis were pushed toward the richly documented units,
many cases would be jettisoned, or comparisons would be
undertaken that in most cases would provide no information.
If one moved toward the lowest common denominator, a good
deal of information would be sacrificed. Some form of multilevel analysis, Tilly suggested, would help to meet the difficulty. A large sample could be drawn, for which sketchy

information could be assembled at low cost. In this case the researcher might be in a position to draw a small, unbiased subsample on the basis of which to assemble detailed information. Three sorts of analyses would ensue: crude analyses of the large sample, fine analyses of the subsample, and comparisons of the fine and crude analyses for the subsample alone. This procedure would give the researcher some grounds for generalizing the results of the fine analysis of the subsample to the entire sample.

4. Problems of dealing with multiple units of analysis simultaneously

A nagging and ever present difficulty in research on community violence is that most researchers are dealing with more than one unit of analysis at the same time and must reconcile the treatment of the various units with each other and with the data at hand. One should not reduce the analysis to a single type of unit or devise independent analytic procedures for each type of unit. In dealing with contemporary collective violence, a combination of survey research, field observation, and documentary analysis would be more productive than an effort that concentrated on only one of these approaches.

5. The problem of attaching violent action to its context

The toughest methodological problem of all five, in Tilly's estimation, is how to represent and measure the connections that in theory account for the production of a certain variety of collective violence by a certain kind of social situation. The problem assumes serious proportions in temporal and ecological analyses of collective violence. If protest and economic hardship vary together over time (as suggested by R. B. Rose and W. W. Rostow), how can the connection between them be identified? If cities in which Negroes have little representation in politics and police forces also have high frequencies of violent protest, how can the links between the two variables be specified with sufficient confidence to recommend one course of action over another? Tilly suggested that one might test for the existence of the links that may theoretically be expected by further research of another form; watch the correlates of changes in the variables

selected; watch for results of deliberate interventions in the
social arrangements when they occur; or manipulate variables
experimentally to learn whether the effects correspond to
theoretical expectations.

Peter Rossi identified some of the major unresolved
issues in the comparative study of community violence.
These issues included: (1) the concept of community as a
way of making distinctions among social phenomena; (2) problems of data collection, particularly in studying community
elites; and (3) special problems of handling qualitative data.

Rossi's major question about the community concept was
whether the phenomenon being dealt with is one in which
major differences from community to community lie in the
aggregate characteristics of its population, in the compositional nature of the community, or in the structural features
of the community.

Rossi felt that community violence is not likely to be
traceable entirely to structural features of the community.
Community violence, which is a form of collective behavior,
is more likely to be related to characteristics of aggregates
or compositional factors than to structural factors. Thus
research into intercommunity variation in community violence
should be oriented primarily toward characteristics of the
populations of the communities and secondarily toward structural features of the communities.

Rossi expected, however, that as Negro communities
became better organized, civil disorders would be more
controlled and focused on political goals. As organized action replaced spontaneous collective behavior, the structural
features of local communities would be increasingly important.

With respect to data collection problems, the immediate
problem is how to obtain a community sample of reasonable
size at a reasonable cost. The most likely course, Rossi
thought, would be to include cities whose characteristics
allowed maximum emphasis upon some particular dependent
variable, though this strategy would have some serious draw-
backs.

Rossi saw no new development in the offing that would lower the direct labor-cost component in surveying, although the high costs and the need for information would continue to provide incentives for cost-saving inventions.

In conducting sample surveys of the general population, researchers are in the position of knowing what ought to be done but are not always able to command the resources to do it, whereas in surveying elites, researchers know only vaguely what they want to do, though such surveys would be relatively easy to carry out if the researchers knew what they wanted.

Success in interviewing elites, Rossi felt, depends heavily on the skill of the interviewers, and their guidance is an "extension of the principal investigator's intuition, more easily acquired by one's graduate students than by ad hoc groups with diverse backgrounds." In brief, although it is fairly easy to devise a satisfactory sampling procedure for elite surveying, it is very difficult to train associates to conduct interviews as the principal investigator would have conducted them himself.

Rossi described the strategy devised by the Johns Hopkins group that surveyed elites in 15 cities. The interviews were used primarily to characterize the community; thus all the information on selected topics was culled from each interview with data pools for each city. Next, a number of variables were devised to represent what seemed important to distinguish among cities. Third, at least three separate raters were used to read the protocol excerpts on each topic and to place the cities in rank order along each of the dimensions to be distinguished. Finally, the end result was a set of rank orders, one each for the major dimensions along which the structural features of the cities were contrasted.

Rossi felt that because excerpts from interview protocols could be characterized according to attributes of the respondent that could be related to the quality of the interview data from that respondent, it should be possible to raise the reliability of the rating task appreciably by restricting the ratings to data of better quality.

This strategy would be useful to apply to any set of qualitative interviews, with better-quality interviews producing correspondingly more reliable ratings. The advantages of this strategy were said to lie in relative objectivity, minimal selectivity of analysts, and provision of a base for quantitative comparisons among cities. Such a strategy would depend heavily on having sufficient cases to sustain the analysis; a number (N) of 15 would barely be sufficient.

TOPICS FOR FURTHER DISCUSSIONS

Discussions about future workshop topics revealed a sharp division between those who wanted to give priority to questions of research techniques and methodology focused on social conflict and collective violence, and those who wanted to emphasize questions of desirable social change: the scholars vs. the social activists. The activists condemned riot research that was directed at improving the mechanism of social control. The scholars insisted on the legitimacy of objective analysis and the importance of improving research methods that would maximize the validity of findings.

"The Lemberg Center is interested in studying violence," John Spiegel noted.

We are not interested in changing a name just because somebody happens to be sensitive to it. In psychiatry, when people began to think that mental illness was a bad word, everything had to be called mental health, but they continued to study mental illness. These discussions are supposed to be on the subject of how one does research in the area of civil disorder. I don't think that our mission is to find the answers for all the problems of the social system, or to make some prescriptions for action in general with respect to what is wrong with the social system, but rather to develop better research methods than we have had so far on civil disorder as a response to the problems in our society. Civil disorder has been too long ignored, and we haven't developed a good way of

studying it. We don't have to be able to predict
what kind of civil disorder we're going to have,
but we have to develop methods for working in
tense situations and being able to capture rapidly
moving social situations. This is something we
haven't done; social science has been terribly
static.

Two separate conferences might be necessary--one to
discuss what kinds of questions researchers should be asking,
the other to deal with methodology. One participant said:

If you're interested in doing something with the
data, you don't have to wait for better, more
sophisticated, and more refined means of studying the situation. A lot is already known and
isn't being acted on for a variety of reasons. I
would be interested in knowing why that is the
case, and that is a separate issue from methodology and involves different kinds of objectives,
goals, and perhaps even people. We are much
farther behind with that problem than with the
problem of methodology.

Some participants urged that future workshops might be
focused on substantive findings of research projects rather
than on methodology, because problems of methodology probably will reveal themselves as one comes closer to the conclusion of the study and begins to wrestle with the data, inter-
pret, and conceptualize the findings.

HOW CAN BLACK SOCIAL
SCIENTISTS BE INVOLVED?

Although there is a definite need for participation of
black social scientists in these workshops, there is no certain means of accomplishing this goal. There was a consensus that future workshops should involve a greater participation by black social scientists, and extra efforts should be
made to insure this participation. Moreover, the workshops

should be structured so that substantive responses to "white-determined" research projects are given full ventilation.

With regard to the responsibility of the scholarly community to bring black social scientists, including aspiring young black social scientists, into the group, a black participant doubted that this would happen in the very near future in the study of violence. He felt that it was intimidating for black social scientists to attend such conferences. "When black people are able to structure these conferences in the main and get the large grants, then they'll feel more attuned to the situation, but now they feel it's white people, once again, studying black people, and they just don't like this sort of thing."

An attempt might be made to help black social scientists in relatively lesser-known organizations to get the kind of research funds that will allow them to organize whatever research they want to do. Possibly this would be a topic to explore at a future conference. Another possibility would be to get black and white social scientists together expressly to mull the questions of what kinds of research ought to be done on community social change, what way researchers should go about doing it, what role the communities ought to play in the research itself, and how money should be channeled for such projects.

A black social scientist warned that it would be difficult to persuade young black people, or old ones for that matter, to become involved. A white participant pointed out that a large investment was to be made in the next few years by both government and private foundations in social science and studies of social change, and black social scientists ought to be heavily involved, but he did not think this could be done on a separatist basis. "I'm keenly interested in direct involvement. I think a lot of the social change that occurs in the United States in the next generation or two is going to be directly relevant to what we call the racial conflict, and blacks have to be directly involved. We have to get over this particular hump."

If there were two conferences--one on methodology and another on basic social questions--the blacks could be large contributors in the second one to an understanding of the situation of the Negro in the United States and might be able to suggest research that could be done to illumine it.

A black participant explained that black social scientists ask where the white researchers on violence were when the Little Rock incident happened, and where the white researchers were when violence was done to Negroes in Selma, Montgomery, and Birmingham?

APPENDIX A

APPENDIX A EXCERPT FROM "A GUIDE FOR ANALYSIS OF COLLECTIVE CONFLICT IN LARGE-SCALE SOCIAL CHANGE"*

A "political disturbance" is an instance of mutual and collective coercion within an autonomous political system that includes violence to persons or property and threatens the existing control over the organized means of coercion within the system. What follows is an explication of that abstract definition.

COLLECTIVE COERCION

One formation of at least 50 persons must be present, representing either the forces of rebellion or the forces of repression. This has been done mainly as a practical measure, because larger groups are more likely to be reported and relevant information is more readily available on them in the sources.

However, for over half of our incidents, no exact or appropriate number of participants is reported. We have decided to adopt a list of words that are often used to describe the incidents, and we are tentatively <u>assuming</u> that they mean the involvement of a large group of people (over 50).

<u>multitude</u>   <u>révolte</u>
<u>rassemblement</u>   <u>rébellion</u>
<u>réunion</u>   <u>insurrection</u>

---

*By Louise and Charles Tilly.

foule	émeute
attroupement	échauffourée
troupe	bagarre
désordre	tumulte
trouble	

If an incident meets the criteria of damage or violence (below) and no number of participants is given, we include it in the sample if it is described by one of these terms. This does not mean that these are the only terms that could be used (e.g., incident, manifestation, agitation, sédition, rixe, bouleversement, fête), but the ones we have chosen imply the participation of a relatively large group of people. We are not using these terms to determine the extent of violence but only as an indicator of participation.

Adjectives of size used with these words are important. Thus, any adjective suggesting a large size (rassemblements nombreux, foule immense) means it is included. Diminutives (petite foule) keep the incident out of the sample.

This excludes any independent violent activity undertaken by an individual or a small group of individuals. Thus we do not include assassinations, murders, thefts, or other crimes committed by less than 50 people (or a group defined by other than one of our collective terms). However, we include violence by a group on the periphery of a larger demonstration. This also excludes action by unknown persons such as sabotage, bombs, or fires. We take these into account, but they are not to be included in the basic sample.

MUTUAL

This means that there must be at least two antagonistic formations involved. However, one may be involved by the proxy of its property or symbols. We include any opposition to the symbols or representatives of authority or another group. Violence must be directed at someone else; thus, workers attacking a newspaper office are included, whereas farmers destroying their own produce in protest against government farm policies are not.

VIOLENCE TO PERSONS OR PROPERTY

Any dead or wounded make the incident qualify. The major problem cases involve resistance to police when it is not clear whether anyone was hurt (stones thrown at troops or mounted gendarmes surrounded by a mob). Seizure of persons without physical injury is also a problem. In general, if persons are seized over resistance, that is enough.

We include any damage done by one group to someone else's property by attacking or seizing control of it. Besides significant destruction, this includes broken windows or symbolic minor damage. It does not include damage to one's own property (farmers destroying own crops, merchants burning their own records in protest), and it must be done by a group--which excludes sabotage, fires, bombings of unknown origins. Seizure of property includes taxation populaire--the forcible seizure of grain or other foodstuffs, followed by their public sale at a proclaimed "just price." It also includes nonviolent occupation of buildings such as sitdown strikes.

These criteria clearly exclude any large political gatherings that do not end in violence or crowds which shout threats of violence but take no action.

WITHIN AN AUTONOMOUS POLITICAL SYSTEM

This is in the definition in order to exclude war and border incidents. It also excludes any violence within such closed institutions outside the general political sphere as prisons, asylums, and hospitals. If individuals break out of these institutions, however, they must be included. We have decided to include army mutinies because the members of the armed forces are part of the political community; a mutiny on a ship would present special problems, depending on its proximity to France.

THREATENS THE EXISTING CONTROL

One of our assumptions is that any violence threatens
the existing forces of control to some degree; thus, this is
the biggest problem. If the incident meets all the criteria
described above, we include it as a potential threat to control. However, certain types of violence that do not have
any political objectives will still get into our sample. Thus
we are not able to eliminate student hazing and rampages,
rixes and fêtes between rival nonpolitical groups, barroom
brawls, or spectator events that break out into violence. We
have decided to include them if the other criteria are met
and identify them as special cases that can be included, elim-
inated, or discussed separately in the analysis.

BOUNDARIES OF DISTURBANCES

When one of the actions just discussed has occurred, we
must set some limits on the events to be recorded and analyzed with regard to time, space, and personnel. When two
or more such actions occur, we must also decide whether
they are parts of the "same" disturbance, or whether they
are parts of related ones. A disturbance begins when at
least two of the formations taking part in the violent action
begin a continuous interaction and ends when the last two formations end their continuous interaction. It occupies all the
space in which a spectator could directly observe the interaction without benefit of mechanical devices. The participants are all persons who perform the crucial action(s), all
persons who interact with them directly in the course of that
action, plus all persons acting collectively with members of
either of the first two categories in the stream of activity
including the crucial action(s). Finally, sets of participants
fall into separate formations to the extent that they act collectively, communicate internally, oppose other sets of participants, and are given distinct identities by observers.
Where we do not have enough information to apply these definitions with any rigor--which is often--we accept the conventional observer's identification of actors, stage, and action.

When two violent actions occur on the same day or on consecutive days, in the same commune or in adjacent ones (in Paris, Lyon, or Marseille--the same quarter or adjacent ones) and there is a reasonable presumption of an overlap of personnel equal to 10 per cent or more of the participants in the smaller action, both actions count as part of the same disturbance, and all of the intervening time belongs to the disturbance. Three or more violent actions with such connections may compound into disturbances covering longer periods and larger territories.

Two disturbances are distinct but linked when they occur in the same or consecutive months, and meet any of these conditions:

1. Concerted action of at least one formation in one disturbance with at least one formation in the other.

2. Strong evidence of overlap in personnel.

3. Strong evidence of the provision of material assistance by the participants in one disturbance to the participants in the other.

4. Overt imitation of the action of one disturbance by a formation in another.

5. Overt response as indicated by demands, slogans, or ritual acts. Three or more disturbances may be linked in this way.

SUMMARY

In summary, the procedure involves six steps: (1) Scan the sources for violent actions; (2) having located a violent action, determine whether the event of which it is a part meets the definition of "political disturbance"; (3) if it does, set its boundaries in space, time, and personnel; (4) identify the formations taking part in the disturbance; (5) determine whether it is linked to any other disturbances; (6) code. To carry out these procedures, the researcher employs the following guidelines:

A. Violence

    1. One dead
    2. One wounded
    3. Any damage to property
    4. Seizure of control of property over resistance

B. Collective

    1. At least 50 persons in one formation (direct evidence through numbers of participants wounded or arrested)
    2. Indirect evidence of a large group through the use of a collective terminology:

multitude	révolte
rassemblement	rébellion
réunion	insurrection
foule	émeute
attroupement	échauffourée
troupe	bagarre
désordre	tumulte
trouble	

C. Mutual

    1. Two formations in conflict
    2. A formation versus an individual
    3. A formation versus property or symbols representing another group

D. Exclude

    1. Sabotage, bombings, fires set by unknown persons
    2. Assassinations, murders, criminal activities by individuals
    3. Large gatherings where no violence breaks out even if they threaten violence
    4. Rebellions within closed institutions: prisons, hospitals, asylums
    5. Symbolic damage to one's own property

E. Boundaries

  1. Begins with continuous interaction of at least two
      formations
  2. Ends with termination of continuous interaction of
      last two formations
  3. Occupies space within which spectator could observe
      interaction directly
  4. Participants: performers of violent acts, others
      interacting directly with them, plus others acting
      collectively with either of the first two groups
      (divided into formations)

F. Multiple Violent Actions Forming Single Disturbance

  1. Same day or consecutive days
  2. Same commune or adjacent communes (in Paris,
      Lyon, and Marseille--same quarter or adjacent
      quarters)
  3. Overlap in personnel of 10 per cent or more of the
      participants in the smaller action

G. Distinct but Linked Disturbances

  1. Same month or consecutive months
  2. Concerted action of formations
  3. Overlap in personnel
  4. Provision of material assistance
  5. Overt imitation
  6. Overt response by demands, slogans, ritual acts

BIBLIOGRAPHY

Charles Tilly

BIBLIOGRAPHY

Charles Tilly

Editors' note: This bibliography was prepared by Professor Tilly to accompany the paper he gave at the Themis House Workshop. Therefore, the choice of items to some extent reflects his particular work on early industrial conflict and his special concern with problems of definition, documentation, and relating violent action to its social context. By general agreement, however, this list of references was found useful in one way or another to every serious investigator of collective violence.

Revolution, Protest, and Internal War

Alroy, Gil. The Involvement of Peasants in Internal Wars. Princeton, N.J.: Princeton University, Center of International Studies, 1966.

Amann, Peter. "Revolution: A Redefinition," Political Science Quarterly, LXXVII (March, 1962), 36-53.

Arendt, Hannah. On Revolution. New York: Viking Press, 1963.

Blanksten, George I. "Revolutions," in H. E. Davis (ed.), Government and Politics in Latin America. New York: Ronald Press, 1958.

Boulding, Kenneth E. Conflict and Defense. New York: Harper & Row, 1962.

Brinton, Crane. The Anatomy of Revolution. New York: Norton, 1938.

Canetti, Elias. Crowds and Power. London: Gollancz, 1962.

Clark, S. D. Movements of Social Protest in Canada.
Toronto: University of Toronto Press, 1959.

Cobb, Richard. "The People in the French Revolution,"
Past and Present, XV (April, 1959), 60-72.

Cobban, Alfred. The Social Interpretation of the French
Revolution. Cambridge, England: Cambridge University
Press, 1964.

Crozier, Brian. The Rebels: A Study of Post-War Insurrec-
tions. London: Chatto and Windus, 1960.

Darvall, Frank O. Popular Disturbances and Public Order
in Regency England. London: Oxford University Press,
1934.

Davies, James C. "Toward a Theory of Revolution," American Sociological Review, XXVII (February, 1962), 5-19.

Davis, Natalie Z. "Strikes and Salvation at Lyon," Archiv
für Reformationsgeschichte, XXVII (1965), 48-64.

Eckstein, Harry. Internal War: Basic Problems and Approaches. New York: Free Press, 1964.

Edwards, Lyford P. The Natural History of Revolutions.
Chicago: University of Chicago Press, 1927.

Farre Morego, M. M. Les atentados sociales en Espana.
Madrid: Artes Graficas, 1922.

Friedrich, Carl J. (ed.). Revolution. New York: Atherton
Press, 1966.

Geschwender, James. "Social Structure and the Negro Revolt:
An Examination of Some Hypotheses," Social Forces, XLIII
(December, 1964).

Gluckman, Max. Order and Rebellion in Tribal Africa. New
York: Free Press, 1963.

Grüll, George. Bauer, Herr and Landesfurst: Sozialrevolu-
tionare Bestrebungen der Oberosterreischen Bauern von
1650 bis 1848. Graz: Böhlhans, 1963.

Hobsbawm, E. J. Primitive Rebels. New York: Frederick
A. Praeger, 1963.

Hoffer, Eric. The True Believer: Thoughts on the Nature of
Mass Movements. New York: New American Library, 1951.

Hopper, Rex D. "The Revolutionary Process: A Frame of
Reference for the Study of Revolutionary Movements,"
Social Forces, XXVIII (1950), 270-79.

Huntington, Samuel P. "Patterns of Violence in World Politics," in Samuel P. Huntington (ed.), Changing Patterns of
Military Politics. New York: Free Press, 1962.

Jackman, Norman. "Collective Protest in a Relocation Center," American Journal of Sociology, LXIII (November,
1957), 264-72.

Johnson, Chalmers. Revolutionary Change. Boston: Little,
Brown, 1966.

Kerr, Clark, et al. Industrialism and Industrial Man. Cambridge, Mass.: Harvard University Press, 1960.

Lieberson, Stanley and Silverman, Arnold. "The Precipitants
and Underlying Conditions of Race Riots," American Sociological Review, XXX (December, 1965), 887-98.

Lissak, Moshe. "Selected Literature on Revolutions and
Coups d'Etat in the Developing Nations," in Morris Janowitz
(ed.), The New Military. New York: Russell Sage Foundation, 1964.

Mack, Raymond W., and Snyder, Richard C. "The Analysis
of Social Conflict--Toward an Over-view and Synthesis,"
Journal of Conflict Resolution (1957), 221-48.

Marx, Karl. The Civil Wars in France. Available in many
editions.

_____. The Eighteenth Brumaire of Louis Bonaparte.
Available in many editions.

Mather, F. C. Public Order in the Age of the Chartists.
Manchester, England: Manchester University Press, 1959.

Meisel, James H. Counter-Revolution: How Revolutions Die
New York: Atherton Press, 1966.

Miyamoto, S. Frank. "The Process of Intergroup Tension
and Conflict," in Ernest W. Burgess and Donald J. Bogue
(eds.), Contributions to Urban Sociology. Chicago: University of Chicago Press, 1964.

Moore, Barrington, Jr. Social Origins of Dictatorship and
Democracy. Boston: Beacon Press, 1966.

Morrison, Denton E. "Relative Deprivation and Rural Discontent in Developing Countries: A Theoretical Proposal."
Prepared for the Annual Meetings of the American Associa-
tion for the Advancement of Science, Washington, D.C.,
December 27, 1966.

Nieburg, H. L. "The Threat of Violence and Social Change,"
American Political Science Review, LVI (December, 1962).

Pettee, George S. The Process of Revolution. New York:
Harper & Row, 1938.

Pinkney, David. "The Crowd in the French Revolution of
1830," American Historical Review, LXX (October, 1964),
1-17.

Ridker, Ronald G. "Discontent and Economic Growth," Economic Development and Cultural Change, XI (October, 1962).

Rimlinger, Gaston V. "The Legitimation of Protest: A Comparative Study in Labor History," Comparative Studies in
Society and History, II (April, 1960), 329-43.

Rose, R. B. "Eighteenth-Century Price Riots, the French
Revolution, and the Jacobin Maximum," International Review
of Social History, III (1959), 432-45.

Rudé, George. The Crowd in the French Revolution. New York: Oxford University Press, 1959.

Rudolph, Lloyd I. "The Eighteenth-Century Mob in America and Europe," American Quarterly, XI (Winter, 1959), 447-69.

Schelling, T. C. The Strategy of Conflict. Cambridge, Mass.: Harvard University Press, 1960.

Smelser, Neil J. Theory of Collective Behavior. New York: Free Press, 1963.

Stone, Lawrence. "Theories of Revolution," World Politics, XVIII (January, 1966), 160-76.

Street, David, and Leggett, John C. "Economic Deprivation and Extremism: A Study of Unemployed Negroes," American Journal of Sociology, LXVII (July, 1961), 53-57.

Tannenbaum, Frank. "On Political Stability," Political Science Quarterly, LXXV (1960), 161-80.

Tilly, Charles. The Vendée. Cambridge, Mass.: Harvard University Press, 1964.

Walter, E. V. "Violence and the Process of Terror," American Sociological Review, XXIX (April, 1964), 248-57.

Walzer, Michael. The Revolution of the Saints. Cambridge, Mass.: Harvard University Press, 1965.

Willer, Michael, and Zollschan, G. K. "Prolegomenon to a Theory of Revolutions," in G. K. Zollschan and Walter Hisrch (eds.), Explorations in Social Change. Boston: Houghton Mifflin, 1964.

Zagorin, Perez. "The Social Interpretation of the English Revolution," Journal of Economic History, XIX (September, 1959), 376-401.

Strike Activity

Cass, Millard. "The Relationship of Size of Firm and Strike Activity," Monthly Labor Review, LXXX (November, 1957), 1334-44.

Chamberlain, N. W. The Impact of Strikes: Their Social and Economic Costs. New York: Harper & Row, 1954.

Clegg, H. A. "Strikes," Political Quarlerly, XXVII (July-September, 1956).

Forschheimer, K. "Some International Aspects of the Strike Movement," Bulletin of the Oxford University Institute of Statistics, X (1948).

Galambos, G., and Evans, E. W. "Work-Stoppages in the United Kingdom, 1951-1964," Bulletin of the Oxford University Institute of Economics and Statistics, XXVIII (November, 1966).

Geotz-Girey, Robert. Le Mouvement des grèves en France. Paris: Editions Sirey, 1965.

Goodman, J. F. B. "Strikes in the United Kingdom: Recent Statistics," International Labor Review, XCV (May, 1967), 465-81.

Gubbels, Robert. La grave, phénomène de civilisation. Brussels: Institut de Sociologie, Université Libre, 1962.

Herlihy, Ann J., and Willis, Daniel P. "Analysis of Work Stoppages During 1954," Monthly Labor Review, LXXIII (May, 1955).

"Incidence and Duration of Industrial Disputes," International Labor Review, LXXVII (May, 1958), 455-68.

Knowles, K. G. J. C. "Strike-Proneness and Its Determinants," American Journal of Sociology, LX (November, 1954).

_____. Strikes: A Study in Industrial Conflict with Spe-
cial Reference to British Experience. Oxford, England:
Basil Blackwell, 1947.

Kuhn, James W. "Strikes and Australia's Industrialization,"
Australian Quarterly, XXVIII (September, 1966).

McCarthy, W. E. J. "The Reasons Given for Striking,"
Bulletin of the Oxford University Institute of Economics
and Statistics, XXI (1958).

Peterson, Florence. Strikes in the United States, 1880-1936.
Washington, D.C.: Bureau of Labor Statistics, 1938.

Rees, Albert. "Industrial Conflict and Business Fluctuations,"
Journal of Political Economy, LX (October, 1952).

Ross, Arthur M., and Hartman, George W. Changing Patterns of Industrial Conflict. New York: Wiley, 1960.

Taft, Philip. "Violence in American Labor Disputes," Annals
of the American Academy of Political and Social Science,
CCCLXIV (March, 1966).

Turner, H. A. The Trend of Strikes. Leeds, England:
Leeds University Press, 1963.

Weintraub, Andrew R. "Prosperity versus Strikes: An
Empirical Approach," Industrial and Labor Relations
Review, XIX (January, 1966).

Quantitative Studies of Protest
and Collective Violence

Bodart, Gaston. Losses of Life in Modern Wars. Oxford,
England: Clarendon Press, 1916.

Feierabend, Ivo K., and Feierabend, Rosalind L. "Aggressive Behaviors within Politics, 1948-1962: A Cross-
National Study," Journal of Conflict Resolution, X (September, 1966), 249-71.

Grimshaw, Allen D. "Urban Racial Violence in the United States: Changing Ecological Considerations," American Journal of Sociology, LXVI (September, 1960), 109-19.

Gurr, Ted, and Ruttenberg, Charles. The Conditions of Civil Violence: First Tests of a Causal Model. Princeton, N.J.: Princeton University, Center of International Studies, 1967.

Hovland, Carl, and Sears, Robert. "Minor Studies in Aggression, VI: Correlation of Lynching with Economic Indices," Journal of Psychology, IX (1940), 301-10.

Kort, Fred. "The Quantification of Aristotle's Theory of Revolution," American Political Science Review, XLVI (June, 1952), 486-93.

Mintz, Alexander. "A Re-Examination of Correlations between Lynchings and Economic Indices," Journal of Abnormal and Social Psychology, XLI (1946), 154-60.

Mitchell, Edward J. Land Tenure and Rebellion: A Statistical Analysis of Factors Affecting Government Control in South Vietnam. Santa Monica, Calif.: RAND Corporation, 1967.

Penrose, L. S. The Objective Study of Crowd Behavior. London: Lewis, 1952.

Rapoport, Anatol. Fights, Games and Debates. Ann Arbor: University of Michigan Press, 1960.

Richardson, Lewis F. Statistics of Deadly Quarrels. Pittsburgh: Boxwood Press, 1960.

Rostow, W. W. The British Economy of the Nineteenth Century. Oxford, England: Clarendon Press, 1948.

Rummel, Rudolph J., and Tanter, Raymond. "Dimensions of Conflict Behavior within Nations," Journal of Conflict Resolution, X (March, 1966), 65-74.

Russet, Bruce M. "Inequality and Instability: The Relation
of Land Tenure to Politics," World Politics, XVI (April,
1964), 442-54.

_____, et al. World Handbook of Social and Economic Indi-
cators. New Haven, Conn.: Yale University Press, 1964.

Singer, J. David, and Small, Melvin. "National Alliance
Commitments and War Involvement, 1815-1945," Peace
Research Society Papers, V: Philadelphia Conference
(1966), 109-40.

Sorokin, Pitirim A. Social and Cultural Dynamics, Vol. III:
Fluctuations of Social Relationships, War, and Revolution.
New York: American Book Co., 1937.

Tilly, Charles, and Rule, James. Measuring Political Up-
heaval. Princeton, N.J.: Princeton University, Center
of International Studies, 1965.

Urlanis, B. Voini i narodo-naselyenie Evropi. Moscow:
Izd. sotisialno-ekonomicheskoy literaturi, 1960.

Wright, Quincy. A Study of War. Chicago: University of
Chicago Press, 1942.

ABOUT THE CONTRIBUTORS

RALPH W. CONANT

is Associate Director, Lemberg Center for the Study of
Violence, Brandeis University (Waltham, Massachusetts).
He previously was Assistant to the Director at the Joint
Center for Urban Studies of Massachusetts Institute of
Technology and Harvard University. Dr. Conant has
lectured at Boston College, University of Denver, New
York University, and Brandeis. He is very active in
professional organizations, including service on the
Regional Health Advisory Committee, U.S. Department
of Health, Education and Welfare; and secretary, Governor's Advisory Committee on Housing and Urban Renewal,
Commonwealth of Massachusetts. Mr. Conant is the
author of The Politics of Community Health and was edi-
tor of The Public Library and the City. His articles
have appeared in Urban Affairs Quarterly, Library Journal Perspective, and The International Journal of Health
Education. He holds a Ph.D. degree from the University
of Chicago.

MOLLY APPLE LEVIN

is a Research Associate, Lemberg Center for the Study
of Violence, Brandeis University. Mrs. Levin formerly
was with the War Labor Board in Washington, D.C. and
later with the U.S. Department of Labor, writing about
collective bargaining practices during World War II while
in these positions. She then turned to radio broadcasting,
writing and broadcasting the daily Woman's Page of the
Air for Station WASA in Havre de Grace, Maryland. She
has written various publications for the U.S. State Department and the Department of Defense and did studies and
writing concerning Title III of the Elementary and Secondary

Education Act for various towns in Massachusetts. Mrs. Levin was educated at the University of Minnesota.

JOHN P. SPIEGEL, M.D.

is Director, Lemberg Center for the Study of Violence, and Professor of Social Psychiatry in the Florence Heller Graduate School for Advanced Studies in Social Welfare. He formerly was an Associate Clinical Professor of Psychiatry at the Harvard University Medical School and lectured in the Department of Social Relations at Harvard. During World War II, he was a psychiatric consultant to the 12th Air Force in the Mediterranean Theatre and Chief of Psychiatric Services in the Air Force Convalescent Hospital in St. Petersburg, Florida, and Spokane, Washington. Dr. Spiegel is the author of Men Under Stress and is co-author (with Roy R. Grinker) of War Neuroses. He has published numerous articles on behavior under stress, family interaction and mental health, and collective violence in urban settings. Mr. Spiegel received his training in medicine at Northwestern University and in psychiatry at Michael Reese Hospital in Chicago and with the Chicago Institute for Psychoanalysis.

CHARLES TILLY

is Professor of Sociology and History at the University of Michigan. He previously was on the faculty at the University of Delaware, Princeton University, Harvard University, Massachusetts Institute of Technology, and the University of Toronto. He was also a Fellow of the Center for Advanced Study in the Behavioral Sciences. For many years, Mr. Tilly has studied urbanization, political conflict, and collective violence. He has published two books: The Vendée, and Race and Residence in Wilmington, which examined housing segregation in an American city. Mr. Tilly holds a Ph.D. degree in Sociology from Harvard University.

PETER H. ROSSI

is Chairman, Department of Social Relations, Johns
Hopkins University. A specialist in urban politics and
social stratification, Mr. Rossi previously served as
Director of the National Opinion Research Center (Uni-
versity of Chicago); on the faculty of the University of
Chicago (Department of Sociology) and Harvard Univer-
sity (Department of Social Relations). In addition, he
did research for the Center for Field Studies, Graduate
School of Education of Harvard, and for the Bureau of
Applied Social Research of Columbia University. Dr.
Rossi has contributed to numerous books; his own books
include Why Families Move, The Politics of Urban
Renewal, and Between Black and White. His articles
have appeared in Public Opinion Quarterly, American
Journal of Sociology, Harvard Educational Review,
Sociometry, American Sociological Review, and Daedalus.
Mr. Rossi has a Ph. D. degree from Columbia University.